The Futures of Prudence

THE FUTURES OF PRUDENCE

Pure Strategy
and
Aristotelian and Hobbesian Strategists

by

NATHAN D. GRUNDSTEIN
Professor, Management Policy
Weatherhead School of Management
Case Western Reserve University

A Zeus Book:

Enterprise Achievement Associates
Hudson, Ohio

A Zeus Book/This edition of *The Futures of Prudence* published by arrangement with the author.

The name "Zeus Book" and the stylized with statue of Zeus and block design are trademarks belonging to Enterprise Achievement Associates.

Library of Congress Cataloging in Publication Data

Grundstein, Nathan D.
  The futures of prudence.

  "A Zeus book."
  Bibliography: p.
  Includes index.
  1. Strategy (Philosophy)—History. 2. Prudence—
History. 3. Aristotle. 4. Hobbes, Thomas, 1588–1679.
I. Title. II. Title: Pure strategy and Aristotelian
and Hobbesian strategies.
B105.S68G78 1984   110   84-13566
ISBN: 0-930305-00-0

FIRST EDITION

© Nathan D. Grundstein, 1983 Library of Congress TXU150-527

   Copyright retained by the author. All rights reserved. No part of this book may be reproduced or transmitted in any form, or by any means, electronic or mechanical, including photocopying, recording, or by any information storage and retrieval system, without permission in writing from the author.

To All Those

Who

Do Something for Virtue

"*The presence of the single virtue of prudence implies the presence of all the moral virtues.*"

Aristotle—The Nicomachean Ethics, *Bk VI, p. 207 (F. H. Peters Transl., Kegan Paul, Trench & Co., 1884)*

"In the conduct of life, the great matter is, to know before hand what will please us, and what pleasure will hold out. So far as we know this, our choice will be justified by the event. And this knowledge is more scarce and difficult than at first sight it may seem to be; . . ."

"All that can be said is, that there remains a presumption in favour of those conditions of life, in which men generally appear most cheerful and contented. For though the apparent happiness of mankind be not always a true measure of their real happiness, it is the best measure we have."

Paley, William—*The Principles of Moral and Political Philosophy* 1785
    (11th American Edition, Richardson & Lord, Boston 1825) pp. 39-40

❋   ❋   ❋   ❋   ❋   ❋   ❋   ❋

"Ah! so may thy seed sometime have rest," I prayed him, "solve the knot which has here involved my judgment.

It seems that you see beforehand what time brings with it, if I rightly hear; and have a different manner with the present."

"Like one who has imperfect vision, we see the things," he said, "which are remote from us; so much light the Supreme Ruler still gives to us;

when they draw nigh, or are, our intellect is altogether void; and except what others bring us, we know nothing of your human state.

Therefore thou mayest understand that all our knowledge shall be dead, from that moment when the portal of the Future shall be closed."

Alighiere, Dante—*The Divine Comedy*, Canto X, (The Carlyle-Wicksteed Transl., Modern Library, Paperback ed., Random House 1950) pp. 56-57.

❋   ❋   ❋   ❋   ❋   ❋   ❋   ❋

"All animals, except men, live with the aid of appearances and memory, and they participate but little in experience; but the race of men lives also by art and judgment."

Aristotle's Metaphysics (Transl. and Comm., Hippocrates G. Apostle, Indiana University Press 1966) p. 12 BkA

The Pattern of The Trilogy

The Futures of Prudence is the second volume of a planned trilogy. The first volume is titled *The Managerial Kant.** The third volume of the trilogy will be a work on *An Artificial Intelligence of Strategy.*

The first volume explored the comparative foundations of the natural intelligence of human reason and the artificial intelligence of the distributive structure of organization reasoning.

The second volume, *The Futures of Prudence*, introduces the concerns of the strategic into the foundations of human reason and is a treatise on the natural intelligence of strategic reasoning and judgment.

The planned third volume will be an inquiry into the foundations of an artificial intelligence of strategy.

*Grundstein, Nathan D.—*The Managerial Kant: The Kant Critiques and The Managerial Order* 1981. (Weatherhead School of Management, Case Western Reserve University, Cleveland, Ohio)

ACKNOWLEDGMENTS

I am twice indebted to Linda Natal, capable office manager of the Division of Managerial Studies at the Weatherhead School of Management. There is, for one thing, the matter of her prowess with the equipment of modern office technology. I would place first, however, her careful, accurate and effective transformation of an old-fashioned, handwritten, draft manuscript—with all of its' calligraphic and linguistic and editorial complexities—into neatly printed pages.

Ann Drain, in her position as Acting Director of the Frieberger Library of Case Western Reserve University during the period when this treatise was being written, provided assistance whenever needed and she continued to indulge me in the use of library resources.

That same indulgence was again extended to me by Paul U. Gallagher and Vera Parker, who deftly manage the John Dewey Library of Johnson State College in Johnson, Vermont.

Anita Rogoff, talented Director of Art Education at Case Western Reserve University, took time out from a busy schedule to create the stylized **Z** with statue of Zeus and block design.

The publication of *The Futures of Prudence*, as was the case with *The Managerial Kant*, has been made possible by the support and encouragement of a number of friends. Once again, but now with respect to the second volume of a planned trilogy, a special statement is thereby warranted through which to acknowledge my indebtedness to them. They are individuals with whom ties of friendship have emerged from out of the exploration of certain ideas. These are ideas the significance of which for personal development is that they invest the professional career in management with more than drab and disposable utilitarian beliefs. It is, thus, a support and encouragement sourced in the richness of enduring relationships that were focused on thinking about what enterprise leadership both demanded of human intelligence and, in turn, contributed to the advancement of that intelligence.

Not all of these are relationships that originated in the context of graduate professional education for management. The practicing professional life has its own share of serendipity, and I acknowledge my indebtedness to those friends whose support and encouragement of *The Futures of Prudence* is sourced in their own professional ideals.

Charles D. Barnes	Gerald D. Kisner
Daniel T. Carroll	Susan L. Manring
John L. DeNinno	Howard R. Maier
Ann Decker	David M. Maysilles
Michael Decker	Tommy J. McCuistion
Douglas C. Eadie	John B. Olsen
Janet B. Eadie	James E. Reynolds
Walter H. Griggs	Richard V. Robinson
Jonathan P. King	Kathryn E. Wilt

I take particular note of long standing ties with John B. Olsen, corporate strategist and (along with Douglas C. Eadie) advisor on strategy to state governments, who moves between boardroom and classroom with ease. The two of us have often banged each other about in frontal strategies of attack and defense with reference to ideas that were, or that might have been, expounded in this treatise.

Richard L. Osborne, Executive Dean of The Weatherhead School of Management, again provided me with knowledgeable counsel and again made available the assistance of the Center for Management Development and Research. As was usual with our encounters, the pleasures of the association far outweighed the seriousness of whatever concerns I may have had.

Once more a special note of indebtedness is due to Theodore M. Alfred, who was Dean of the Weatherhead School of Management during the years when this treatise—and the years when the predecessor volume—were being written. It is not just that he used his powers to ease the conditions for the writing of these two treatises. There is his understanding that the development of professional competence in the management of complex institutions is furthered by including in management education that which management philosophy can contribute to management science.

I would be remiss were I not to acknowledge the intellectual legacy of Professor Spencer D. Parratt, who was my mentor during the graduate years spent at The Maxwell School of Citizenship and Public Affairs of Syracuse University. It was due to him that the idea of the regulative in human affairs was firmly implanted in my mind. He examined the regulative as both technique and design in a constitutionally structured telics for control of human interests. At a later time I was awakened to the pervasiveness of the regulative in the workings of the human mind itself, and to the significance of the idea of the regulative for a comprehension of those workings. The Hobbesian "Trayn of Regulated Thoughts", which is one of the centerpieces of *The Futures of Prudence*, leads to strategic thinking as a particular kind of regulative intelligence with respect to the future. The idea of the regulative encompasses not only the question of what is that regulative intelligence. It also encompasses the question of what is the intelligence of the regulative? They are questions that drive the search for explanation into metaphysics as well as empirics.

Finally, I abandoned my spouse for the secret pleasures of authorship, but as she is no stranger to my literary desertions, she understood everything and continued to provide me with support and sustenance.

PERMISSION TO REPRINT

The publishers of the works of authors who are cited in the bibiliography have been generous in their granting of permission to quote. There follows a list of the publishers and the authors and the works, for excerpts from which, permission to reprint has been given.

Alighieri, Dante *The Divine Comedy* (The Carlyle-Wicksteed Transl., Random House, New York, Modern Library, Paperback ed., 1950) Reprinted by permission.

The Nicomachean Ethics of Aristotle (F. H. Peters, Transl., Second ed., Kegan, Paul, Trench & Co., London 1884) Reprinted by permission of Routledge & Kegan Paul, Ltd., London)

Aristotle's Metaphysics (Hippocrates G. Apostle, Transl. and Comm., Indiana University Press, 1966) Reprinted by permission of Hippocrates G. Apostle and The Peripatetic Press, Grinnell, Iowa)

Aristotle on Coming-To-Be and Passing-Away (E. S. Forster, Transl., Harvard University Press, 1955)

Aristotle *Parva Naturalia,* "De Memoria et Reminiscentia" (W. D. Ross, ed., Oxford University Press, 1955) Reprinted by permission.

Aristotle's Physics (W. D. Ross, Transl. and Comm., Oxford University Press, 1930) Reprinted by permission.

Aristotle De Anima (R. D. Hicks, Transl. and Notes, Cambridge University Press, 1907) Reprinted by permission.

Bergson, Henri *The Creative Mind* (Maybelle L. Andison, Transl., Philosophical Library, New York, 1946) Reprinted by permission.

Bergson, Henri *Matter and Memory* (Allen and Unwin, London 1911) Reprinted by permission of George Allen & Unwin, Ltd., Hemel Hempstead.

Bohr, Niels *Atomic Physics and Human Knowledge* (John Wiley & Sons, 1958) Reprinted by permission of Mrs. Margrethe Bohr, Copenhagen, Denmark, and The Niels Bohr Institute.

Evans, J. D. G. *Aristotle's Concept of Dialectic* (Cambridge University Press, 1977) Reprinted by permission.

Flew, Anthony *Hume's Philosophy of Belief* (Routledge & Kegan Paul, Ltd., London 1961) Reprinted by permission.

Fraser, J. T., Haber, F. C. and Mueller, G. H. (Eds.) The Study of Time: *Proceedings of the First Conference of the International Society for the Study of Time* (Springer-Verlag, New York, 1972) Reprinted by permission.
 A—Denbigh, K. G.—"In Defence of the Direction of Time"
 B—Watanabi, Satosi—"Creative Time"

Fraser, J. T., Laurence, N. and Park, D. (Eds.) *The Study of Time III: Proceedings of the Third Conference of the International Society for the Study of Time* (Springer-Verlag, New York 1978) Reprinted by permission.
    A—Denbigh, K. G.—"The Objectivity or Otherwise of the Present"
    B—Toda, M. "The Boundaries of the Notion of Time"
    C—Merleau-Ponty, J.—"Ideas of Beginnings and Endings in Cosmology"
    D—Turner, F.—"Poiesis: Time and Artistic Discourse"
Harre, Rom *The Principles of Scientific Thinking* (University of Chicago Press, 1970) Reprinted by permission.
Harre, R. *Matter and Method* (MacMillan & Co. Ltd., London, 1964) Reprinted by permission.
Heidegger, Martin *What Is Called Thinking* (Harper & Row, New York 1968) Reprinted by permission.
Heidegger, Martin *Existence and Being* (H. Regnery Co., Chicago, 1949) Reprinted by permission of Regnery Gateway, Inc., Chicago.
Heidegger, Martin *On Time and Being* (Joan Stambaugh, Transl., Harper & Row, New York 1972) Reprinted by permission.
Heidegger, Martin *The Question Concerning Technology* (William Lovitt, Transl. and Intro., Harper & Row, New York, Colophon Books 1977) Reprinted by permission.
Heidegger, Martin *Being and Time* (John Macquarrie and Edward Robinson, Transl., SCM Press Ltd., London 1962) Reprinted by permission.
Heidegger, Martin *Kant and The Problem of Metaphysics* (J. S. Churchill, Transl., Indiana University Press 1962) Reprinted by permission.
Heisenberg, Werner *The Physicist's Conception of Nature* (Arnold J. Pomerans, Transl., Hutchinson & Co. Ltd., London 1958) Reprinted by permission.
Heisenberg, Werner *Physics and Philosophy* (Harper and Brothers, New York 1958) Reprinted by permission of Harper & Row, New York.
Henderson, Laurence J. *The Order of Nature* (Harvard University Press, 1917)
Hobbe's Leviathan (Reprint, edition of 1651, Oxford University Press 1909, Imp. of 1929) Reprinted by permission.
The Philosophical Works of Descartes (E. S. Haldane and G. R. T. Ross, Transl., Vol. I, 1911 Ed. reprint, Cambridge University Press, 1931) Reprinted by permission.
Kant, Immanuel *The Doctrine of Virtue* (M. J. Gregor Transl., Harper & Row, New York, Torchbook, 1964) Reprinted by permission.

Marcel, Gabriel *Presence and Immortality* (Michael A. Machado, Transl., Duquesne University Press, 1967) Reprinted by permission.

Martha Craven Nussbaum *Aristotle's De Motu Animalium* (copyright © 1978 by Princeton University Press, Excerpt, Chapter 7) Reprinted by permission.

Owen, G. E. L. *Aristotle on Dialectic* (Oxford University Press, 1968) Reprinted by permission.

Pflug, Gunter "Inner Time and The Relativity of Motion" in Gunter, P.A.Y. (ed.), *Bergson and the Evolution of Physics* (University of Tennessee Press, 1969)

Shepard, Paul *Thinking Animals: Animals and The Development of Human Intelligence* (Viking Press, New York 1978) Reprinted by permission of the author.

Smith, Homer William. Reprinted by permission of New York University Press from *Homer William Smith: His Scientific and Literary Achievements* edited by Herbert Chasis and William Goldring. Copyright © 1965 by New York University.

Tiryakian, E. A. (Ed.) *Sociological Theory, Values, and Socio-Cultural Change* (Free Press, Glencoe, Ill. 1963) Reprinted by permission of MacMillan Publishing Co., Inc., New York.

CONTENTS

FOREWORD   xxi

PREFACE: A Theory of Pure Strategy   xxvii
    Pure and Practical Strategy
    Pure Strategy
    Pure Strategy and Material Reality
    Pure Strategy, Causality and Material Reality
    Pure Strategy, Causality and Time
    Matter and Strategic Cognition: Hobbesian Strategist
    Modalities of Cognition: Aristotelian Strategist
    Matter and the Aristotelian Strategist
    Mechanism, Teleology and Strategic Cognition
    Hobbesian Materialization of Reason and Thought
    Being
    The Future as Alternative Materialization
    Strategic Futures as Cosmology
    Burdened and Unburdened Prudence

CHAPTER I: The Prudentiality of Prudence   1
    Aristotelian Prudence
    Hobbesian Prudence
    Prudence, Virtue and Wisdom

CHAPTER II: Prudence as Thought and Action:
              Hobbesian Prudence   6
    Regulated Thought as Mechanism
    Desire and Designe

Possessory Certitude and Prudence
Causality and Hobbesian Prudence
Natural Relation and the World for Action
The World as Hobbesian Spectacle
Possessory Certitude and the World for Action

CHAPTER III: Prudence as Thought and Action:
                Aristotelian Prudence   17
Prudence, Sensibilization and Desire
Desire, Purpose and Practical Reasoning
The Thatness and Whatness of Prudence
Non-Possessory Certitude and Prudence
Volition and Prudential Purpose
Virtue, Volition, Reason and Prudence

CHAPTER IV: Prudence as Other-Than-Action   26
  1: Sensibilization, Imagination and Thought
    Imagination: Hobbesian
    Thought: Hobbesian
    Enmattered Thought
    Aristotelian Sensibilization
    Imagination: Aristotelian
    Thought: Aristotelian
    Imagination and Action: Deliberative Imagination
    Thought and Imagination: Hobbesian and Aristotelian

CHAPTER V: Prudence as Other-Than-Action   38
  2: Deliberation and Inwardness: The Hobbesian Prudent
    Designe
    Desire Itself
    Inwardness
    The Passions
    The Felicity Driven Actor
    Past and Future in Deliberation
    The Practical Imagination

CHAPTER VI: Prudence as Other-Than-Action   46
  3: Deliberation and Inwardness: The Aristotelian Prudent
    Prudence, Deliberation and Purpose
    Virtue, Prudence and Deliberation
    Virtue, Prudence and "The Good"
    Reciprocal Subjectivity and Subjectivity Itself
    Prudence, Deliberation and Dialectics

CHAPTER VII: Prudence and Strategies of Thought   60
    The Materiality of Knowing
    Substance and Sensibles
    Event Time and Psychological Time
    Strategy of Thought

CHAPTER VIII: Being-in-the-World and the Hobbesian Actor   68
    The Triple Chain of Material Causality
    Differentiation Between Actors
    The Passions, Subjectivity and Materialization
    Time, Desire and Thought
    The Reason That Reckons
    The Future As A Fiction of the Mind
    Prudence As Post-Calculative Cognition
    Hobbesian Being-In-The-World

CHAPTER IX: Being-in-the World and the Aristotelian Actor   82
    The Three Questions of Materiality
    Overknowing and Virtue
    Underknowing and Overknowing
    Knowing and Materiality
    The Aristotelian Potencies
    The Hobbesian Potencies
    Formative Potency
    The Formative Potency of the Aristotelian Prudent
    Virtue, Possessory and Non-Possessory Orders

CHAPTER X: Being and Prudential Knowing   93
    Being and Subjectness
    Being and Knowing
    Being As A Pre-Emptive Potency
    Being and Prudence
    Volitional Time and Fateful Thinking
    Hobbesian "Seeing" and Calculative Thinking
    Passionate and Meditative Thought
    Virtue, Passionless Thought and Prudential Knowing
    The Good
    Calculative Materialization
    The Good of Moral Virtue

CHAPTER XI: The Worldhood of Prudence   108
    1: Worldhood Without Nature
        Blind Nature and Purpose Serving Events

Memory and Recollection
   Hobbesian Causality
   2: Worldhood With Nature
   Nature as Telic Causality
   Actuality, Potentiality and Matter
   Actuality, Potentiality and Action
   Chance and Purpose-Serving Events
   3: The Duality of Futures
   Actuality, Potentiality and Change
   Designe, Potentiality, and Futures

CHAPTER XII: Prudence and the Worldhood of Temporality 121
   Action and Time-Space Coding
   The Actor As Entity Within the World
   Cognized Time
   Intentive Time

CHAPTER XIII: The Future as Hobbesian Prudence 128
   The Past As Powerlessness
   The Past As Consciousness
   The Past As Expectation
   The Present As Actuality and Pre-Figuration
   The Psychologizing of Time
   The Perceptual Consciousness of Prudence
   The Being of the Present
   The Future As Desire

CHAPTER XIV: The Future as Aristotelian Prudence 138
   The Transformation of Desire Into Thought
   The Future As Thought
   The Future As Imagination
   The Future as Practical Intellect
   Aristotelian and Hobbesian Materiality
   Eductive Representations: The Aristotelian Imagination
   The Future As Pre-Formation
   Kinematic and Kinetic Materiality

CHAPTER XV: The Times of Time 149
   Heterogenic and Homogenic Time
   Event Time
   Social Time As Event Relational Time
   The Time of the Agent of Action

The Temporality of An Order
  Orderless Temporality

CHAPTER XVI: The Futures of Prudence   159
  Futures As Cosmology
  Futures As Cosmology Forward and Cosmology Backward
  Hobbesian Prudence: Cosmology Backward
  Prudence and Wisdom
  Aristotelian Prudence: Cosmology Forward
  Prudential Good As Gnostics
  Futures As Potentiality and Actuality
  Contained Futures and the Future As An Abandoned
    Present
  The Intrusive Future of Being

BIBLIOGRAPHY   171

INDEX   175

FOREWORD

The Futures of Prudence is a work of exploration and explanation of the natural intelligence of strategy. It is a work the origins of which are to be found in the exposition by Aristotle and by Hobbes of the cognitive foundations of prudence. In their separate expositions of the idea of prudence, Aristotle, and also Hobbes, provide the first templates of the natural intelligence of human actors as strategists. Strategy, like Aristotelian and Hobbesian prudence, reaches around to include the interaction of knowledge and interests. The templates of strategy, like the templates of Aristotelian and Hobbesian prudence, are templates of a structure for knowing and of a structure of knowledge.

Taken together, they lead to an explanation of strategy as strategic cognition. The structure of strategic knowing and the structure of strategic knowledge are the cognitive structures of strategic thinking. They are the natural intelligence of strategic actors. The explanation of strategy in terms of these cognitive structures is the object of *The Futures of Prudence.*

The path of cognitive explanation leads to a theory of pure strategy. In a theory of pure strategy, all operationalism is put to one side. Instead, the basic cognitions are put in issue. The cognitions of strategy function as transformational linkages between a strategic actor and the world for action. Strategic cognizing on the part of the strategic actor is sourced in an infrastructure of human materiality. And the world for action is a world made material through sensibilization. The materiality of the strategic actor, and the materiality of the world for strategic action, join to bring to the fore an underlying thematic of explanation for strategic cognition. It is a thematic that emerges from the conjunction with conceptions of material reality that originate in physics and in metaphysics.

They are conjoined in the systematic philosophies of Aristotle and Hobbes. Theirs are philosophies in which are contained the referent first principles from which are derived the cognitive structures of the natural intelligence of humans. Hobbes, like Aristotle, was endowed with an intellect that was capable of setting forth an inclusive systematic philosophy. Hobbes was impressed by the discoveries of Galileo concerning motion, and bodies. He placed Galileo at the apex of the "age of natural philosophy". Hobbes's *Elements of Philosophy* contained a considerable amount of physics, which he termed "the phenomena of nature." In the *Elements* he set forth a systematic treatment of the elements of natural philosophy—time, place, cause, power, relation, proportion, quantity, figure, motion, sensory phenomena, the world and the stars, and gravity. All of this was preceeded in the *Elements* by discourses on method, on syllogism's, and on "ratiocination of the mind."

Hobbes's treatise on *Human Nature* was also meant to be a further extension of referent first principles of a philosophy of "Faculties, acts, and passions." It was a treatise in which there was a detailed exposition of imagination, memory, intellect, cognitive and conceptive powers, motives to action, will, the passions, sense faculties and knowledge, experience, thought, and conceptions of the future.

Aristotle, too, had ranged in his thinking and writing over a terrain of fundamental principles regarding the world, cosmology, the phenomena of nature, and the knowledge of man. The terrain covered by Aristotle was as wide and as broad as that traversed by Hobbes. Each of the two, moreover, had singled out prudence for special treatment. Even beyond that, each had nested prudence in those first and fundamental principles by which they had explained the natural intelligence of humans and

Foreword

the world of existence. Each set prudence firmly within a particular structure for knowing and a particular structure of knowledge. The fundamentals of the cognitive structures for strategic thinking, power, and action were thereby established, for they have their origins in the cognitive foundations of prudence.

Nevertheless, comprehension of the notion of the strategic in modern terms requires still another turn at the cognitive foundations. The basic cognitions must once again be put in issue. *The Futures of Prudence* puts these cognitions in issue as the method by which to achieve a comprehension of strategic intelligence. They are put in issue by placing in opposition Aristotelian and Hobbesian theories of prudential knowing.

A prefatory chapter introduces the notion of a theory of pure strategy. It then goes on to examine the relevance for strategic cognition in such a theory of certain conceptions of material reality that originate in physics. The metaphysics of materiality has its own special relevance for strategic cognition. Chapters VII, VIII, and IX are centered on the special relevance of conceptions of material reality that are to be found in metaphysics.

The distinctiveness of prudential knowing as a structure of knowledge with transformational power as respects a desired future actuality is set out in Chapter I. Science and wisdom are differentiated from prudential knowing. What remains, nevertheless, as a connection between them?

The explanation of cognitive structures for knowing, and for the directionality of knowing, by Hobbesian and Aristotelian strategists begins with Chapter II and Chapter III. The Hobbesian and the Aristotelian structures are placed in opposition to one another. The two cognitive structures are shown to be differently linked to different directive foundations of reasoning, of ways of thinking, of purpose and "designe", of volition and choice, and of causality and action.

The three chapter sequence starting with Chapter IV examines the Aristotelian and Hobbesian other-than-action of prudence. This other-than-action is the domain of inwardness, the domain within an actor. The imagic and imagination provide a first path of entry. The second is the path of linkage between desire and "designe". The passions provide a third path of entry. The exercise of volitional choice also lies within the domain of inwardness. What characterizes the other-than-action of prudence is the interpretation of the constitutive and the regulative of prudential (strategic) knowing.

The material fundament of knowing—the physicality of matter as an explanation of the foundation structures of knowledge—is the focus of both Chapter VII and Chapter VIII. What are strategies of thought and how are they possible? This question is the central concern of Chapter VII. What are the chains of material causality by which the prudential (strategic) actor establishes the stance from which the world of external materiality will be known? This question is the central concern of Chapter VIII. It is also the central concern of Chapter IX, but now the question is explored in terms of the Aristotelian explanation of the material fundament of knowing.

Being and prudential knowing is the centerpiece of Chapter X. Subjectness and knowing; subjectness and the directionality of thinking emerge as the essence of Being. It leads into knowledge of the formative potency by which there can be created an order of things in the world as an actuality of existence. Modes of thinking, and conceptions of time, and the introduction of virtue into the gnostics of prudence are traced to their origins in Being. How it is that primary differences between Aristotelian and Hobbesian prudents (strategists) are sourced in Being is explained.

The existential concept of Worldhood supplies the gravity center around which revolves the content of Chapter XI and Chapter XII. What is the explanatory cognizing of the materiality of the world for action that enters into a physical explanation of prudential action itself? Brought to the fore by the concept of Worldhood is experiential time—the understood temporal order in which events present themselves in experience. There is an interlocking of the chain of causality in time, and of purpose-serving events and efficient cause. The structuring elements of Worldhood with (Aristotelian) and without (Hobbesian) nature are disclosed.

Foreword

In Chapter XII, however, Worldhood and temporality are singled out for analysis. There is the way in which human thought has ordered the world for action in terms of time-space coding. The cognitive implications of the prudential (strategic) actor as a time-binding entity within-the-world are detailed. The concepts of cognized and intentive time are introduced.

The way has now been prepared for an extended inquiry into the epistemology of futures. A future is an epistemological construct. The future as Hobbesian prudence is the substance of Chapter XIII. The future as Aristotelian prudence is the substance of Chapter XIV. In Chapter XV the times of time are elaborated.

Futures as cosmology is the culminating chapter of this treatise on the futures of prudence. The formative potency of prudential (strategic) knowing lies in its capability to generate transformational knowledge. In turn, transformational knowledge enters as a power of causality into the Aristotelian coming-to-be-and-passing away. Aristotelian prudence has put forth an epistemological envelope of futures as an invisible metamorphic of the coming-to-be-and-passing away of orders of things in the world. Each such order in relation to the formative potency of prudence exists as a metamorphic order—subject to change or causing change in form, in structure, or in substance of the order itself.

An order of things in the world is a material order of existence, however much it is sourced in the knowingness of the prudential. The formative potency of prudential knowingness is thus, a cosmoplastic potency. Futures are invested with cosmological attributes. The "thinking of thinking" that is the ultimately regulative of Aristotelian prudence, also turns it to the obligation of wisdom with respect to an order of things in the world as an actuality of human existence.

References

The English Works of Thomas Hobbes of Malmesbury, (Sir William Molesworth, Ed., John Bohn, London, 11 Vols. 1839-1845)

Nathan D. Grundstein
May 1984

PREFACE

A Theory of Pure Strategy

Pure and Practical Strategy

THE PRESENT WORK is an inquiry into pure strategy. The notion of pure strategy is not a familiar one. It is, rather, the empirics of practical strategy and the pragmatics of praxis in strategizing that are familiar as the knowledge of strategy. Nevertheless, the idea of pure strategy should not be surprising. Reason itself has been divided into pure reason and practical reason. (1) It has long been established that each is a fertile domain for cognitive inquiry. So, too, may the field of strategic knowledge be separated into the domain of pure strategy and the domain of practical strategy.

A theory of strategy would include both a theory of pure strategy and a theory of practical strategy. Pure strategy consists of conceptions alone. Practical strategy consists solely of the empirics of strategizing. The task of a theory of pure strategy is to disclose the conceptions that underlay the empirics of practical strategy. The knowledge of practical strategy is focused on the empirics of operations, of processes, of information and data bases, of analytic methods, of decision structures, of planning and change, of implementation, and the like. For all empirics such as these, however, there is a foundation of antecedent strategic knowledge. It is the conceptual fundament that is the substance of strategic cognition. The final achievement of a joinder of conception and empirics in a theory of strategy is an artificial intelligence of strategy.

Pure Strategy

Pure strategy is the cognitive envelope of the knowledge for all specific strategies. The knowledge that is the capability by which it is possible through human agency to introduce causality into a future order of things in the world is the cognition of pure strategy. The causal power with respect to a future is strategic capability.

A concern with pure strategy is a concern with explaining the human power of futures making. Pure strategy has its origins in the conceptions of prudence elaborated by Aristotle and by Hobbes (the anti-Aristotelian). As the grand theorists of prudence, they invested it with powers of explanation for that which is generated by human agency to be as a future in human affairs. The futures of prudence are the original indicators of the futures of pure strategy. The conceptions of pure strategy delve once again into the primary questions of futures making.

What are futures?
What is strategy that it has a power of futures making?
What is strategic thinking?
What becomes of time?
What is strategic causality?
What explains strategic choice?

Pure strategy involves conceptions of the causal agency of human thought and action, but these conceptions proceed from a more fundamental ground of explanation. In pure strategy, strategic capability confronts the enigma of the reality of matter for the strategist. Materiality underlies all the empirics of strategy,

Preface

starting with the necessity of the strategic actor to confront his own materiality. Pure strategy begins with conceptions of materiality, with conceptions of what the strategist utilizes to interpret the experienced materiality of existence in the world. A future as an order of things in time is necessarily an order whose foundation locks into the reality of matter in time. In pure strategy, what is critical for strategic cognition is to determine what that reality is, and what constitutes the relation of the strategist to material reality.

The strategist conceptualized as the agent of causality, and regulating cognition and volition in the context of the materiality of the world for action, is the starting point for a theory of pure strategy. So conceptualized, the strategist of pure strategy is linked by the history of thought to explanatory suppositions of cognition and matter that have their origins in the speculative materialism of Zeno, and that re-appear as the scientific materialism of Newton. So conceptualized, moreover, the strategist of pure strategy is also linked by the history of thought to explanatory suppositions of mind, perception, understanding, ends, reason, assent (choice), volition, and agency (*praxia*) that were first elaborated within and about the doctrines of the academists of ancient Greece. (3)

Pure Strategy and Material Reality

At the outset, then, a doctrine of some sort concerning matter enters into a theory of pure strategy. Matter contains the realty for strategy, but what is the reality of the material—material reality—for the strategist? The physicist, more than the strategist has developed an acute consciousness about conceptions of matter. It is from these that the physicist constructs physical conceptions of nature.

Physics was once dominated with conceptions of matter "by two great conceptual systems . . . The Aristotelian and The Newtonian." (2:7) These two concepts of matter are introduced into strategic thought through Aristotle and Hobbes, each of whom theorized about strategy as prudence. It is in this perspective that strategists can be comprehended as Aristotelian and Hobbesian actors.

Strategists are not physicists. However, the self-conscious questions about their concepts of matter that are the concern of physicists are questions that have relevance for strategists. It is not just for physics that questions of relationality between an actor and material reality have significance. In the observational empirics of the 17th and 18th centuries, relationality was without explanatory significance. The actor was a passive observer of nature as an objective material reality. Since then radical alterations have taken place in the conceptualization of the relationship between nature (material reality) and an actor.

In the history of physics, the empiricism of the 17th century, the empiricism that underlay the mechanical sciences—and that is exemplified by Newton—excluded, as incompatible with its model of the perceptual world, all dependence of the reality of matter on the Being or essence (quiddity) of an acting subject. Not to exclude would mean that there was "no independent, causally active world." (2:45) Heisenberg has put it, however, that with the coming of atomic physics "the last objective reality" has disappeared, and that the "common division of the world into subject and object" became inadequate for an understanding of the physical world, or nature. (4:24)

Decisive changes in the character of technology—from the mechanical to the electro-technical and chemical and atomic technologies—transformed what was once understood to be nature. The ensuing technological surround with which the actor equips himself, however, is not viewed by Heisenberg as belonging to *nature*. Technical instrumentation is likened by him "as the snail's shell is to its occupant or as the web is to the spider. . . . a part of our organism rather than parts of external nature." (4:18) What is left for physics as one of the exact sciences is not "a picture of nature so much as a *picture of our relationships with nature*." (4:29)

Preface

Pure Strategy, Causality and Material Reality

For a theory of pure strategy, the difference between cause in the maximum sense and cause in the minimum sense is central to relationality between the strategic actor and material reality. The Hobbesian actor begins from the stance of a passive observer, which is a stance that encases the materiality of the world within "a minimal sense of causation". (2:15) What causation in this sense has been said to mean for physics is precisely what it can be said to mean for the Hobbesian strategist:

> (i) The cause-event or phenomena is an observable occurrence and so is the effect-event or phenomenon; but the relation between them is not an observable event or occurrence. This follows from a general philosophical position expressed in the principle: 'All we can observe in a serial change are the events which severally compose it.' (2:15)

As observer, the Hobbesian actor does not attempt to explain phenomena, but he does accept their material foundation. Phenomena are connected up in the sensibilized experience of the strategist as actor, but there is no resort to theoretical concepts to mediate the observed relationships between phenomena.

Simply as perceptual experiences, there is an absence of *praxia* or agency on the part of the Hobbesian actor. It is only with the introduction of the idea of the causal agency of human action that "the maximal sense of causation" is introduced as the core concern of the strategist. Again, what causation in this sense has been said to mean for physics is precisely what it can be said to mean for the Hobbesian strategist.

> (i) . . . There is the idea of agency or productivity of the effect by the cause—the cause together with the conditions in which it acts generates the effect.
> (ii) Each answer is open, since we can continue to expand it by giving more details of the mechanism by which the causal agent produces the effect . . .

> (iii) Each answer is a list of necessary conditions for the occurrence of the effect, or at least each answer can be treated in this way, for each element in an answer mentions a feature of the situation which is of such a kind that if it were absent the effect would not occur. But no answer, however expanded, contains sufficient conditions for an effect, since the list of necessary conditions is open. (2:14)

The Hobbesian prudent or strategist is interested in what his present power enables him to control as an actor. Hence the core concern with causation in its maximal sense. Hence, also, an admission that no causal connection between antecedent and consequent in a serial succession of events could be asserted. Hence, finally, the importance of experience to the Hobbesian prudent. The Hobbesian strategist is brought back to consider that which is presently within his power and by which to achieve a future good. The strategist as an agent of causality supposes

> that some selection of the set of necessary conditions . . . can be made which will suffice for the practical production of the effect against a background of relative stability in all other conditions . . . (2:15)

Pure Strategy, Causality and Time

The conceptions of causality and causal agency bring pure strategy into conceptions of time. The concept of time is also one which has given physicists some difficulty. The difficulties have their origins in the shift of the matter that is the concern of physicists—the shift from "the quantum theory of the atomic shell" (relatively slow moving) to "high-energy elementary particles" (velocity nearly that of light). In the mechanics of Newtonian physics, the structure of space and time was such that time as past, present and future could be described as follows:

> If we describe all those events as past of which, at least in principle, we can obtain some knowledge, and as future all those events as which, at least in principle, we can still have some influence, then

according to our naive conception we believe that between these two types of events there is but one infinitely short moment which we call the present. This was just the conception on which Newton had based his mechanics. Since Einstein's discovery in 1905, we know that between what I have just called 'future' and 'past' there exists an interval whose extension in time depends on the distance in space between an event and its observer. Thus, the present is not limited to an infinitely short moment in time. (4:47-48)

The Hobbesian prudent or strategist brings to pure strategy the questions associated with observation as ordinary perception, and the questions associated with information derived from ordinary perception in time. For the Hobbesian strategist, it is a sequence of events in time that gives a practical reality to time. Time consists of the subjective framing of events in a sequence of antecedent and consequent.

However, as to the events themselves in time, they are without duration in time. There is a temporal relationality of nondurational events. Is there a causal foundation for the observed relationality in time? It is a question that is without utility and without relevance for the Hobbesian actor. Sensations do not explain the materiality of the appearance of events. The percepts of contingent perception do not explain any causal ordering of the events of the material world. The actor, in the materiality of his properties and states and processes exists within a non-explicable materiality of events as perceived appearances. Yet the actor is capable of achieving a strategic conception of his powers as an agent of causality in time. (5:28-45)

Matter and Strategic Cognition: Hobbesian Strategist

A theory of pure strategy requires a theory of strategic cognition. There are connections between doctrines of matter and strategic cognition. Given a particular doctrine by which the reality of matter is established, what, then, of the knowledge of an acting prudent, the strategic actor? If the doctrine is that matter is to be defined by the properties that it exhibits (2:7-8, 63), then the knowledge of the strategic actor must depend on the sensibilization of these properties or qualities of matter. Sensibilization is a modality of cognition. It is through this cognitive modality that the strategist tries to move from a minimal sense of causation to a maximal sense of causation. The movement from the one to the other is done by a regulation of thought or cognition.

What that regulation of thought consists of is the hallmark of the Hobbesian prudent or strategist. It is not necessary that the strategist know "what are in fact the fundamental and real properties of the material world." (2:61) It is not even necessary that the strategist separate out the qualities of perception from the properties of matter. Given the quest of the Hobbesian strategist for a maximal sense of causation as the justificatory ground for acting as an agent of causality, what the strategist wants to know is only "regularities of coexistence and regularities of succession." (2:55)

The strategic cognition of the Hobbesian prudent is derived from knowledge of things in the perceptual world. It is a knowledge of regularities that accompany change in their observed arrangement and change in their observed properties as things. The knowledge of experience becomes longitudinal cognition. It serves also as a way of resolving the question of time that is implicit in change. Nevertheless, time emerges as a critical problem for strategic cognition when the modality of cognition is restricted to the sensibilization of the properties of matter.

Modalities of Cognition: Aristotelian Strategist

Are there more and other modalities of cognition than just sensibilization of the properties of things in the perceptual world? The question is an important one for a theory of strategic cognition. Is thought both dependent on the contingencies of representation and limited in its ideas to that which has appeared as a representation of materiality?

The psychology of Aristotle enlarged the concept of thought to include imagination, separating it out from representation. The metaphysics of Aristotle made thought something that generates "final cause"—thought can bring about the occurrence of definite material events as a particular end. Thought thus enters into the maximal sense of causation. Additionally, an Aristotelian distinction is made between an appearance and a sensation. Every appearance is contingent on the person for whom it exists as a particularized appearance. So nothing about the reality of material things can be established simply from appearance or sense based representation. Nevertheless, appearance can give rise to objects of thought—educed representations. Material things can be made intelligible (dematerialized) as objects of thought. The qualities of sensible things, as attributes of materiality, can be abstracted from the form of their materiality and become objects of thought. The independence of cognition from the doctrines of matter has its source in the metaphysics of Aristotle.

Matter and the Aristotelian Strategist

The doctrine by which the reality of matter is established for the Aristotelian prudent or strategist also enters into a theory of pure strategy. Here the reality of matter is to be understood within a "general conceptual system" rather than in terms of empirics. It is that while material things exhibit properties, "there is an underlying unity which persists through radical changes of many of the properties of things. The invariants in natural processes are the items which are material." (2:8)

Not sensibilized matter in and of itself, but matter as form/substance. Matter as form contains properties which, though not themselves accessible to sight, are the generative properties that could be sensibilized and understood in terms of their coming-to-be. In form is the whatness or the quality or the quantity or the whereness of matter. Matter as form/substance—with its generative properties—is linked to Aristotelian concepts of potentiality and actuality.

The linkage is one that provides space for a power of strategic choice with respect to change. Matter both contains its causality—sources of change in its properties—and is also subject to change by an external agent with the causal potency to do so. (6:147, 198 Bk ⊕, △) The causal potency of an external agent is a power of strategic choice—a power comprehended in terms of actuality and potentiality.

Mechanism, Teleology and Strategic Cognition

Aristotelian metaphysics brings strategic cognition behind the empirical curtain of sensibilization. Aristotle introduced mechanism and teleology as "two complementary aspects of things" (7:26), really two forms of causality. Therefore explanation required a searching out of both "the mechanical cause and the reason of everything." (7:20) As to this duality of mechanical causation and teleological causation, Henderson has written:

> But though mechanical causation can readily be abstracted from all teleological views, teleological forms, as Kant thoroughly explained, always involve chains of mechanical causation. Though we can readily separate the mechanical from the teleological nature, we can on no account separate the teleological from the mechanical, if we are to think about it scientifically. So, in spite of Kant, when scientific research employs teleological concepts such as function, adaptation, fitness, or natural selection, it is obliged to regard them as cognate with mechanism and I believe that organization has finally become a category which stands beside those of matter and energy. (7:66-67)

Pure Strategy and Command Cognition

The Aristotelian power of strategic choice makes a particular kind of cognition critical for pure strategy. That cognition may be termed command cognition. Nature may have its ends, for which there is a mechanism of explanation, but the strategic actor introduces a teleology whose mode is that of conscious design or purpose. It is the relation of teleology to cognition that makes command cognition a regulative cognition. Regulative cognition is regulated teleology.

A theory of pure strategy is a theory in search of an explanation of both the cognition of command and its regulativeness. The organic foundation of regulative cognition is to be found in physical biology, where, as Henderson phrased it: "Aristotle's original view of the internal teleology of the living thing, which is nothing more than self-regulation, has completely established itself in physiology." (5:84) The strategic actor as a living organism necessarily introduces organization into the material infra-structure of cognition. To introduce organization is also to introduce regulation, for in physical biology "the concept of regulation is governed by that of organization." (*ibid.*)

The utility of mechanism as an explanation of organic regulation is a special problem of physical biology. A satisfactory ground of explanation for strategic cognition—the cognition that regulates teleology—is a special problem for a theory of pure strategy. Teleological regulation, like organic or biological regulation, also has its mechanism. It is the mechanism of a power—a power of thought.

In the philosophy of the Aristotelian strategist, that which has the power of sensation also has the power of thought—that is, a cognizing intelligence. " . . . *thought* either affirms or denies every object of *thought* or intelligible object." (6:70 BkΓ) Thought may, in its connections between objects of thought, think truly or falsely. Thought may also have as its object " 'a false fact', . . . either what does not exist or an existing thing which creates the appearance of being what it is not." (6:100 BkΔ) Thought also has a productive or generative power. (6:117 BkZ). Thought and choice are linked in the "rational potencies." (6:151 Bk Θ) Choice is linked to a potency for accomplishment. Potency for accomplishment is linked to reason through knowledge, which is reason. It is knowledge that invests science with potency. (6:148 Bk Θ) In sum, reason, generative power, potency, and choice are the components of command cognition as a power of thought.

Hobbesian Materialization of Reason and Thought

The Hobbesian strategist assigns to reason less a power than a utility. He constrains reason to numerical analysis. Reason is so constrained because its function in relation to causal agency is defined for it. It is, in part, defined by the locus of the actor as an agent of causality in the world of material existence. The Hobbesian actor exists and acts within a triple chain of material causality. There is the causal chain of material relationship. There is the causality of the material chain of sensibilized representation. There is the chain of external materiality, the real matter external to the acting agent.

In part, too, the function of reason is defined by "designe". As to "designe", it is more than purpose and more than intention. Designe is causality imagined either as an effect producible through causal agency, or as all imagined and desired effects consequent upon object possession by the acting prudent or strategist. Designe generates and regulates a train of thoughts, infuses it with a particular sensory content, so that thinking becomes the materialization of thoughts.

"Designe" expresses the subjectness of the strategic actor. It is constitutive of strategy as imagined causality and desired effect. It is regulative of thought as the source of possible objects of strategy. It posits nothing of necessity in any association of antecedent and consequent between appearances or representations. But it does frame the context of relationality between the strategist and the sensibilized world of appearance. It is the context of causal agency on the part of the strategic actor; that agency whereby subjectness can be transformed into the power or force to achieve the materialization of a desired future.

The difference between the thought of Aristotelian prudence and the thought of Hobbesian prudence is the difference between the thought that is non-mattered (The Aristotelian differentiation between sensation, appearance and thought) and enmattered thought (The Hobbesian sensibilization of thought). The difference is rooted in the explanatory capacity of materiality with respect to thought. The reproach of the Aristotelian to the Hobbesian strategist is that the latter, in taking care to avoid overknowing, has answered three fundamental questions in a way such that the Hobbesian actor becomes committed to underknowing.

The three questions are: First: How does matter make itself known to other matter? Second: How does matter impose itself on other matter? Third: Why does matter impose itself on other matter?

The Aristotelian actor like the Hobbesian actor has addressed himself to answering these three questions. But the Aristotelian actor has also addressed himself to a more ultimate question, which is: Materiality explains materiality, but what is it of materiality that explains the what of materiality?

Being

Is there no more to be explained than conceptions of causality and causal agency as derivatives of the materiality of both the actor and the world for action? There is the materiality (objectiveness) of the strategic actor as part of the materiality of the world. There is the unknown reality that is the materiality of the world for action, and about which nothing can be asserted concerning its objective attributes *qua* matter. What about Being? For the Hobbesian strategist, Being is an irrelevancy. There is no differentiating essentialness as between strategic actors. They are alike in their powers of sensibilization or responsiveness to matter. They are equal in their power to experience. They are each moved to action by desire and aversion. Nor does Being fit into any of the explanatory mechanisms of reasoning and choosing. Ontological relationships, in short, with the material world are without significance for the Hobbesian strategist.

The Hobbesian strategist works with an implicit notion of subjectness. Too, it is an implicit notion that is too constrained, limited as it is within the mechanism of psychological explanation. The essential nature or quiddity (Being) of the Aristotelian strategist, and the being-in-the-world (existence) of the strategic actor, can take the strategist outside of the frame of the mechanism of psychological explanation of knowing and action. The referent of Being is not physical biology translated into a psychology of integrated actions. Nevertheless, certain puzzles of explanation confront a theory of pure strategy by the location of Being outside of behavioral psychology. Harre—who has concluded that "Basic principles lack background because they are the background for everything else . . ."—has put forth the notion of protolaws:

> A protolaw strives to become a law, by seeking a theory to which to attach itself. In this way it becomes associated with ideas of a generative mechanism which explains the phenomena it describes. (9:132)

There is, furthermore, (again following Harre) the puzzle of demonstrative and recognitive criteria by which to prove the existential—including events, things, substances, attributed powers and properties. There are always questions about the capability of their existing in actuality, but what Harre advocates is an enlargement of traditional logic so as to preserve "the major methodological intuitions of scientists about existence, about laws and about causes." (9:65)

However, it is relationality rather than just phenomena, including the presentation of the world to the actor (rather than its representation by the acting strategist) that has significance for a theory of pure strategy. For the Aristotelian strategist, there is more to materiality than is included within the materiality of the Hobbesian strategist. Moreover, being-in-the-world (existence) infuses into pure strategy more than just the possessory stance towards the world that characterizes the strategy of the Hobbesian actor.

The Future As Alternative Materialization

The futures of pure strategy are the futures of alternative materialization of the world. In the potency whereby to generate alternative materialization of the world is the strategic power of futures making. Alternative materialization of the world is futures making. Alternative materialization of the world carries with it a formative potency with respect to an order of things in the world. The power of alternative materialization also invests the futures of pure strategy with a cosmological quality.

An order of things may be a notion less enigmatic for practical strategy than for pure strategy. In the case of the former, an order of things may be empirically defined in terms of a significant parameter (technological or economic or financial) and noted as a necessary condition to which all "designe" must be subservient. In practical strategy, an order of things, under the conditions of experience, can be understood in its practical particularity. A technological order, to illustrate, may be recognized and accepted as a dominant materialization of the world, one which is chosen by the strategic actor to serve as a frame of the future for a specific strategy. The future presents itself in the present in the form of a defined order of things.

The idea of an order is put forth in the critiques of Kant as an idea of pure reason, a pure conception. Under the conditions of experience, however, an order of things is transformed from pure idea into the particularities of practical idea. An enigmatic quality still adheres to the conception of an order of things, whether as pure idea or as practical idea. As idea it contains, or is imbued by reason, with a certain causality; as causality it has its origins in human agency; as human agency it is a product of human thought and action; as human thought and action it is traceable to the fundaments of cognition and desire and reason and existence. It is the constituents of these and their relationship to the strategic actor that constitute the enigmatic qualities of the conception of an order of things for pure strategy. (10)

The enigmatics of an order are associated with regulative teleology. Inquiry into and explanation of strategy are drawn far beyond the consciously purposive. The domain of regulative teleology includes more than purposiveness. The entry into this domain is through prudence, which provides pure strategy with its explanatory philosophy. The opposition between Aristotelian and anti-Aristotelian philosophies of prudence provide the necessary philosophic base. Aristotle and Hobbes (as the anti-Aristotelian) are the grand theorists of prudence, and hence of pure strategy. It is in the rich explanatory value of their philosophies that there is to be found the understanding by which to relate pure strategy to the enigmatics of an order.

Strategic Futures as Cosmology

In the case of both Hobbesian and Aristotelian strategists, there is a certain psychologizing of the material world. This psychologizing consists of transforming it into constituent elements of subjectness—designe, desire and aversion, thought, calculation, experience, deliberation and volition. There is a mechanism of explanation regarding the acting strategist that is to be found in the essentials of these constituent elements. Hobbesian strategists however, unlike Aristotelian strategists, stop at where this psychologizing of the material world ends. For them it is all that is requisite for the power of causal agency—a present power whereby to obtain some future good. It is sufficient for a possessory stance towards the world, the hallmark of success for which is felicity. What is materialized as a future good, therefore, is also psychologized into its subjectness for the acting strategist. There is, in consequence, the generative cosmoplastics of alternative materialization of the world as an actuality of strategic outcomes, but there is no sense of cosmogonics.

Prudence can take the form of a calculative mode of knowledge, the application of which can yield alternative futures as imagined futures, in the sense of calculated scenarios that are imagined but not yet existent alternative materializations of the sensibilized world. Alternative futures are the particularized products of the analytics of calculation that is practical reasoning. Alternative futures are the stuff of the cosmoplastics of the Hobbesian strategists.

It is not that the Aristotelian strategist is indifferent to the calculative. Indeed, the calculative is recognized and accepted by him as a "kind of reasoning" associated with purposive action. It is the kind of reasoning—practical reasoning—that is resorted to in the relational context of sensibilization, desire and choice. (11:182)

Still, from the perspective of futures as cosmology, dual futures signify something different than alternative futures. Dual futures encompasses both the cosmogonics involving coming-to-be-and-passing-away, and the cosmogonics with which reason itself is concerned. The first includes worldhood with nature. In the Aristotelian view nature is "not generated by choice for the sake of something." (6:188) Nature is a prior cause of things, and within the things that are generated by nature there exists final cause. So nature contains its own telic causality, for within the things of nature are contained the potentiality of all principles of change. Nature itself contains a future.

There is the acting strategists' relation to the elements of potentiality and actuality of this future through purposive action. The acting strategist resorts to calculative reasoning to arrive at that which will be materialized or "generated by choice for the sake of something." (6:188BkK) In the calculative mode of knowing, "*knowledge* and sensation and opinion and *thought* are always of other objects." (6:210BkΛ) The strategist acting within the calculative mode of knowing leaves off any "profound pursuit of causes", to use a Hobbesian phrase. It is a strategic avoidance that is characteristic of worldhood without nature. It is also a deliberate concentration or limitation of thought to the concerns of the actor's personal fortunes.

There is, further, the future generated in consequence of reason itself. Not practical reasoning—a kind of thinking—but the thinking intellect. Reason itself as the thinking intellect is a vault of intelligible comprehension. The Aristotelian strategist has knowledge of the material world both in terms of order and change (its coming-to-be-and-passing-away) and in terms of the intelligible aspects of its materiality. The what of materiality becomes not its appearance as sensibilized representation, but the intelligible aspects of matter. Reason itself is that which is capable of apprehending and thinking in terms of the intelligible. The thought of the thinking intellect is not enmattered thought. Here is the vault of intelligible comprehension.

Reason itself is the source of an intrusive future. It is the source of cosmogony intruding into the material necessity of utilitarian futures. Reason itself is the vault of intelligible comprehension. Intelligibility as a power of reason itself is anterior to representation and appearance, and anterior to calculative reasoning. Reason itself has for its object its own intelligibility; that is, intellect itself. With the intellect as the object of thought, "Thinking is the thinking of thinking." (6:209Bk Λ) Pure strategy, as the cognitive envelope of strategic knowledge, has its own cognitions as its object. Thinking is no longer the enmattered thought of practical reasoning, focused and constrained as the latter is on the objects of desire.

It is also reason itself as the fundament of Aristotelian prudence that introduces Being or ontology into strategic cognition. Aristotelian prudence is taken to contain the expression of "some divine element" in the whatness of Being, and hence in life itself as an element of essential Being in the nature of man. It is reason itself actualized as intellect in life itself, making intelligibility prior in its generative causality to that of sensibilized thought as a cause of something.

Here is the place that Hobbes has fenced around with warnings against inquisitiveness into the causality of events beyond what appeared to be linked to a desired outcome. Thought for the Hobbesian strategist has an exclusively utilitarian concern, and that is its utility for "designe" and for the end of "felicity". Utilitarian concerns lock the strategist into material necessity. Desire itself inclines the strategist to endless acquisitiveness. Each acquisition is both the means to another and the assurance of that already acquired. Desire, "perpetuall and restlesse", transcends time. (11:75)

Burdened and Unburdened Prudence

Hobbesian strategy, therefore, remains an unburdened prudence. It is not burdened by anything beyond its own effectiveness in the achievement of felicity. Aristotelian strategy, however, remains a burdened prudence. It is burdened both by "practical or moral virtue" and by wisdom. The former was ranked inferior to the latter in the attainment of happiness. Moral virtue was "emphatically human", for it is "closely connected with the passions"; and it also required a certain "external good fortune." (8:341-344) It is the conjunction of moral virtues with prudential purpose and action that provide contemplative reason with intuitive and demonstrative knowledge as avenues to wisdom.

REFERENCES

1. The significance for management theory of the separation of reason into pure reason and practical reason by Kant is the subject of a separate work. See Grundstein, Nathan D., *The Managerial Kant* (Weatherhead School of Management, Case Western Reserve University 1981)

2. Harre, Romano—*Matter and Method* (Macmillan & Co., London 1964)

3. *The Morals of Cicero* (Transl. and Intro., William Guthrie, London, 1744)

4. Heisenberg, Werner—*The Physicist's Conception of Nature* (Hutchenson & Co., London 1958)

5. Hanson, Norwood R.—*Observation and Explanation* (Harper & Row, Torchbook ed. 1971)

6. *Aristotle's Metaphysics* (Hippocrates G. Apostle, Transl. and Comm., Indiana University Press, 1966)

7. Henderson, Lawrence J.—*The Order of Nature* (Harvard University Press, 1917) Information subsequently emerged as an additional category.

8. *The Nicomachean Ethics of Aristotle* (F. H. Peters Transl., Kegan, Paul, Trench & Co., London 1884)

9. Harre, Rom—*The Principles of Scientific Thinking* (University of Chicago 1970) " . . . a causal relation obtains when one state of things or substances generates or produces another, and some generative or productive mechanism can be found, or imagined under the license of science, by which the production or generation is achieved." (9:85)

10. Hayek, F. A.—*The Sensory Order* (Routledge & Kegan Paul, London 1952), Hayek, F. A.—"The Concept of Order", in Vol. I, *Rules and Order*, pp. 35-52 of *Law, Legislation and Liberty* (University of Chicago 1973). And see ref. 7, above, (physical biology) and ref. 4, above, (disintegration of the formal order in physics).

11. *Hobbes's Leviathan* (Rep. ed. of 1651, Oxford University Press 1909, Imp. of 1929)

CHAPTER I

The Prudentiality of Prudence

THE WAY OF PRUDENCE LEADS to futures—particular kinds of futures. The futures that emerge from prudence are concealed within the potency of prudence itself. The prudentiality of prudence is potency with respect to time. It is prudence that makes the future one of the times of time. Not time itself; not the future in time, or the time of the future; but the times of time.

The way of Aristotelian prudence leads to one future, while the way of Hobbesian prudence leads to another. How is it that each has its own potency with respect to the future; that the times of time of the one are not the times of time of the other? Inquiry is turned by that question to the gnostics of futures that is concealed within prudence.

Aristotelian Prudence

Prudence is the truth of practical judgment. Not far into his *Metaphysics*, the statement is made by Aristotle that "the end of a practical science is performance." (1:35 Bk A). Given this juncture of performance and prudence in the practical, the prudentiality of prudence is a potency. It is a potency by which there is a power of prudence to create an order of things in human affairs.

It is a potency of thought as well as of action. The truth of prudence materializes as its potency. Its truth as knowledge, however, is of a particular kind. Aristotle put it that "prudence is a formed faculty that apprehends truth by reasoning or calculation, and issues in action, in the domain of human good and ill." (2:18) Prudence, for Aristotle, was indeed a way of thinking associated with acting.

It was precisely because of its special link to action that he differentiated prudence from the other modes of reasoning of which mind was capable. Science was one of these enumerated modes, but, by differentiating prudence as a practical science, Aristotle set off the practical from the theoretical in science. Each had not only its truth, but also its own kind of knowing. Practical science, even though it involves the examination of "how things are" does but "investigate what is relative to something else and what exists at the moment, and not what is eternal." (1:35 Bk A) As against the performance that is the end of a practical science, "the end of a theoretical science is truth."

Aristotelian prudence remains, therefore, on a lower rung of the science of knowing. At the highest rung is "universal knowledge in the highest degree." It is the hardest to know because it is "most removed from sensations." (1:14 Bk A) The rung of prudence has to do with how both the "general truths" of universal knowledge and the "particular facts" of practical knowledge enter into actions of practice. Prudence "issues in action, and the field of action is the field of particulars." (2:192)

Prudence has a special knowledge, which is experience with the particularized or individuated knowledge of sensibilization. It is not that knowledge of "general truths" is not a concern of prudence. It is, rather, that Aristotle fixed the concern of prudence on "matters of practice," or particulars of action. Prudence is not merely the discernment of intelligence.

> . . . for intelligence has not to do with what is eternal and unchangeable, nor has it to do with events of every kind, but only with those that one may doubt and deliberate about. And so it has to do with the same matters as prudence; but they are not identical; pru-

dence issues orders, for its scope is that which is to be done or not to be done; while intelligence discerns merely . . .
"Intelligence, in fact, is equivalent neither to the possession nor to the acquisition of prudence; . . . (2:198)

Whatever it might be as a science, Aristotelian prudence could not be a science of demonstrative truth. As a practical science, however, prudence could infuse action with whatever knowledge was possible by way of a science of the materiality of things subject to sensibilization. What was required of prudence was that it build up a special knowledge of "particular facts", so that, in "the sphere of action", prudence could perform well in dealing with variable and alterable causes or principles.

Hobbesian Prudence

Hobbesian prudence is separated from science, which is considered to be an utilitarian alternative to prudence. The Hobbesian conception of science excludes all that is theoretical. The worth of science is what its usefulness might be for an acting prudent. As between prudence and science, Hobbes concludes that the "signes of prudence are all uncertain" and "the signes of science, are some, certain and infallible; some uncertain." (3:38) In the absence of the certainty of science, "naturall prudence" is to be preferred as the guide to action. Here the preference accorded to prudence was because the knowledge of prudence was the knowledge of ordinary experience; and it was through such experience that the actor would be familiar with the rules by which to apply that knowledge. The knowledge of science was not the knowledge of ordinary experience, but the product of an abstract, deductive method of analysis "attayned by Industry." Prudence had its own observable "signes" whereby to guide present action. For the Hobbesian prudent, who appraised science solely in terms of its utility for present action, prudence, rather than science, might often be placed on a higher rung of knowing.

Prudence, Virtue and Wisdom

Unlike Hobbes, Aristotle did not imprison the prudentiality of prudence in the practical and in sensibilized knowing of the world for action. The Aristotelian position is that

> . . . even if it did not help practice, we should yet need prudence as the virtue or excellence of a part of our nature; and, in the second place, that purpose cannot be right without both prudence and moral virtue; for the latter makes us desire the end, while the former makes us adopt the right means to the end. (2:207)

Aristotelian prudence introduces into prudentiality a presencing virtue that is not a derivative of empirical knowing. It also subordinates prudence to wisdom. Like prudence, wisdom is also a way of thinking, but it is superior in its thinking to prudence. Wisdom unites the general propositions of demonstrative knowledge with a non-calculative knowing of reason. The practical ends of prudential action are subordinate to the interests of wisdom. Their function is to provide "means for the attainment of wisdom." (2:207) The practicality of wisdom is that it does "produce something", for "wisdom being a part of complete virtue its possession and exercise make a man happy." (2:203)

Aristotle doubted that of all things in the universe, man is the best of all. (2:190) The interests of wisdom directed knowledge beyond the personally advantageous to "knowledge of the noblest objects". (2:190) Nevertheless, "prudence, though inferior to wisdom, must yet govern it, since in every field the practical faculty bears sway and issues orders." (2:202)

Hobbesian prudence is unable to discover any relevance of virtue for prudence. Virtue remains unlinked to any regulative mechanism of thought and action. "The secret thoughts of man run over all things, holy, prophane, clean, obscene, grave, and light, without shame, or blame." (3:55) It accepts the governing dominion of the personally advantageous as both fundamental and exclusive in prudential thought and action. All prudential choosing about action is a product of calculative reasoning on the part of an acting prudent.

REFERENCES

1. *Aristotle's Metaphysics*—(Hippocrates G. Apostle, Transl. and Comm., Indiana University Press, 1966)
2. *The Nicomachean Ethics of Aristotle*—(F. H. Peters, Transl., Kegan Paul, Trench & Co., London 1884)
3. *Hobbes's Leviathan*—(Rep. ed. of 1651, Oxford University Press 1909, Imp. of 1929)

CHAPTER II

Prudence as Thought and Action: Hobbesian Prudence

THE EXPLANATION OF THE ACTION of the Hobbesian prudent is in terms of a regulative mechanism from the operations of which action itself is a derivative outcome. To be action, that which follows from "The Trayn of regulated Thoughts" of the Hobbesian actor cannot be just that which emerges from an internal regulative mechanism for action. What emerges from a regulative mechanism for action that is internal to the actor cannot become action in a world that is external to the actor, unless a transition from the internal to the external world is possible.

Regulated Thought as Mechanism

Hobbes introduces the concept of "regulated Thoughts". (1:20) The prudence of Hobbes becomes understandable as an aspect of regulated thought. To be sure, the Hobbesian regulated thought is a way of thinking. The threshold question is: What is thought itself? The concept of regulated thought was accepted by Hobbes only after he had worked through the threshold question. All thought rests upon the immediate sensory data generated by external objects pressing upon the sensory organs. Thought gives rise to representations (appearances) of objects which possess the qualities attributed to them by sensibility, or the sense organs.

Prudence as Thought and Action: Hobbesian Prudence

So, for Hobbes, the world for action exists in a way that is both anterior to and external to the actor himself, and it is a world that appears to the actor as representation or appearance. There is no representation, however, that is not a sensory cognition; nor can anything be cognized that has not previously been sensibilized.

The Hobbesian actor proceeds from sensibilization of both the world for action and the acting agent of action. The world for action consists of sensible matter only. He does not try to account for any intelligibility of the world of material actuality that exists and is known to him through sensibilization. He experiences phenomena as appearance, the reality of which is not known to him. He has no explanatory generalizations about them. The world for action is understood in terms of the contingencies and accidents of its phenomena as experienced by an agent of action.

Desire and Designe

Still, it is possible for an agent of action to have a "Trayne of Thoughts", identified by Hobbes as that succession of thoughts which constitutes "Mentall Discourse." (1:18, 19) It is here that regulated thought makes its appearance, for regulated thought is a "Trayne" of thought "regulated by some desire, and designe". (1:20) As elaborated by Hobbes:

> From Desire, ariseth the Thought of some means we have seen produce the like of that which we ayme at; and from the Thought of That, the Thought of means to that mean; and so continually, till we come to some beginning within our own power. And because the end, by the greatnesse of the impression, comes often to mind, in case our thoughts begin to wander, they are quickly again reduced into the way: (1:20)

Prudence is linked not to desire, but to designe. Both designe and prudence are private to the acting prudent. Each prudent has "his private designes." Each, also, has the privateness of experience. The privateness of designe and the privateness of experience are linked to one another in the consciousness of each prudent. Prudence consists of the "wit" by which one knows, remembers an experienced and patterned complex of observed things, and judges the possibility of designe being achieved. Prudence involves the observational knowing and remembering and judgment of "uncertain signes." It is the occasions of experience that can reduce this uncertainty.

The function of pre-emptive regulation of thought and action is assigned by the Hobbesian actor to "some desire, and designe." (1:20) As pre-emptive regulators, "desire, and designe" constrain the "Discourse of the Mind" to a nondiffused focus for action. Desire leads to an aim and points the thought generated by the possessory imagination to a chain of means that finally settles in a beginning within the power of the actor. Designe is different than desire. Designe refers to a "designe in hand". It is that which takes shape in the mind of the prudent as an opportunity attaching to the directional interlocking of a "multitude of things." The prudent observes what it is that they "may conduce unto", or he observes that they fit into a settled designe that had taken shape prior to their actual occurrence. The Hobbesian world for action exists as a domain of opportunity for an acting agent as an efficient cause.

Designe regulates the "Trayne" of thoughts, or "Discourse of the Mind", in that inventive search or "Seeking" by which there is "a hunting out of the causes, of some effect, present or past; or of the effects, of some present or past cause." (1:20) The world of materiality becomes transformed by perceptual consciousness to a structure of external objects experienced as factual actuality, but subject to laws of material necessity and connection by which, when known, the effects of action can be both forseen and calculated.

It is not necessary for the Hobbesian actor to resort to Reason to explain action. Action has its invisible ground in the "small beginnings of motion" caused by that which sensibility discerns in the external world of materiality. Action begins within the invisibility of the interiority that is "within the body of man." The directive quality of action lies in "Appetite or Desire," by which endeavor moves the actor "toward something which causes it." (1:39) As for the visible act itself, volition alone is enough to account for an act. But will is an act, not a faculty of willing. Act and will are one.

Possessory Certitude and Prudence

The regulated thought of Hobbes is significant as the way of thinking that opens a path to action which, when traversed as thought, brings to consciousness what actions are within our own power." The regulated train of thought turns inward upon the actor. The actor becomes aware of his own circumstances as actor. The actor then comes to judgment about his power; that is, his own capability as an agent of action to obtain that which he would have by desire and designe.

It is the framework of time that gives prudence its utility as thought. If all knowing is sense based cognition of a world that is both prior to and external to the knower, how, then, may one know either the past or the future? Hobbes was quite clear about the ground of such a question.

> The *Present* only has a being in Nature; things *Past* have a being in the Memory onely, but things *to come* have no being at all; the *Future* being but a fiction of the mind, applying the sequels of actions Past, to the actions that are Present; (3:21)

From an action standpoint, certitude with respect to the future is everything. The utility of prudence lies in its certainty function, which Hobbes made a function of experience. "By how much one man has more experience of things past, than another; by so much also he is more Prudent and his expectations the seldomer faile him." (1:21). What Hobbes had done was to locate the human agent of action in a special place with reference to the world for action. Events to come were not viewed as the product of the volition of the actor. All that the actor had was the regulated thought of desire and designe—which, in the context of time, was an expectation in relation to the future and, in relation to the past, "a *re-conning*" or "calling to mind" of the former actions taken by the actor and the events that followed. (1:21) The world for action, however, was conceived as "a world of pure exteriority, a world of elements acting on one another." (2:137)

A world for action which was, by the regulated thought of the human agent of action, made "a world of pure exteriority" limits the thinking of the actor to a certain type of certitude. The regulated thought of the human agent of action leads solely to that certitude which is expected to open to the actor "his present means, to obtain some future apparent Good". (1:66) It is a certitude about his power as a human. This is the certitude of possession, of which Marcel has written:

> To say that I am in quest of a certitude is not enough. What is it that I claim to do with this certitude . . . Will it be necessary to have the notion of power brought in here? If I have the certitude that such an event will take place, I can act accordingly. This certitude confers on me a certain power in reference to this event. I can prepare myself for it, take some precautions, etc. Such a certitude can therefore be possessed in the sense in which one possesses a means for . . . This is also applicable to everything which permits a determinate category of problems to be resolved. (2:149-150)

Hobbes leaves no room for the transformation of the human agent of action as subject. There is neither "utmost ayme" nor "greatest good." There is only desire never ending, "and therefore the voluntary actions and inclinations of all men tend, not only to the procuring, but also to the assuring of a contented life." (1:75) Desire, of course, can be realized only through "present means to obtain some future apparent Good," which is Power. No object is desired in and of itself. Every object of desire is "but the way to" another desired object. Desire, however, transcends every particular object. While there is no "utmost ayme," the object-transcending attribute of desire insures "that the object of man's desire, is not to enjoy once only, and for one instant of time; but to assure for ever, the way of his future desire." (1:75)

The agent of action is thereby extended in time as acting subject by the object transcendence of desire. The world of exteriority—which is the world for action—is thereby extended in time as the certitude derived "from the difference of the knowledge, or opinion each one has of the causes, which produce the effect desired." (3:75) Nevertheless, the acting agent is contained within the finitude of the present, which is the finitude of the actor's present means to obtain some future apparent Good. The object transcendence of desire, by extending the acting subject in time, compels "a perpetuall and restlesse desire of power after power, That ceaseth only in Death." (1:75) The human agent of action is imbued with this "generall inclination" because the human actor is aware that "he cannot assure the power and means to live well, which he hath present, without the acquisition of more." (1:75)

Causality and Hobbesian Prudence

Desire infuses the actor with an active striving for the certitude of possession. To know causality is taken to be the equivalent of the knowledge of a depersonalized objective certitude. Here the "designe" of regulated thought, deliberation, and willing conjoin with the knowledge of causality. The necessity for deliberation arises out of the uncertainty introduced into the thinking of the agent of action by the actor's own Desires (Appetites) and Fears (Aversions) about the consequences of either doing or not doing something which, in the mind of the actor, is a possible outcome of action on his part. Deliberation puts an end to the liberty of the actor doing or not doing in accordance with the subjective imperatives of desire and aversion. Both doing and not doing have their consequences. Deliberation is the prelude to the act of willing. The will that gives rise to voluntary acts is the final outcome of a precedent deliberation. Liberty precedes action. Liberty is the freedom of an actor in relation to the internal imperatives that are grounded in his own appetites (desires) and aversions (fears). Willing is the prior act that enables all subsequent acts of an actor to be voluntary actions.

All this notwithstanding, Hobbes still does not make knowledge of causality the essence of certitude. The point of the matter is that causality is not separable from Hobbesian "designe".

> When the thoughts of a man that has a designe in hand, running over a multitude of things, observes how they conduce to that design; or what designe they may conduce into; if his observations by such as are not easie, or usually, this wit of his is called Prudence; and dependeth on much experience, and memory of the like things, and their consequences heretofore. (1:55)

No level of abstraction about the knowledge of causality could push off the world of pure exteriority from the actor, so as to make the world for action exist independently of, and without relation to, the actor.

Hobbes had arrived at an interpretive position with reference to causality that is reminiscent of the treatment of causality by Hume. The approach to cause by both is such that there is for each a fusion of causation with agency. (3:Ch. 6) It is not only that in the succession of objects or events in time that cause precedes what follows. It is not only that cause has this "temporal priority" in relation to effect. Neither of the two was interested in cause as a descriptive explanation of mechanism located in the world of exteriority. Their interest in cause was practical and utilitarian. Hume had himself written in his *Inquiry* that science taught "us how to control and regulate future events by their causes." Such teaching is utilitarian from the standpoint of the potential agent of action.

> What this does all indicate is the fundamentally practical character of the concept of cause. Causes bring things about. The notions of causation and agency are both encapsulated within the meanings of all transitive verbs. It follows from this that if a cause is one which itself can as a matter of fact be brought about or prevented by human agency then that cause provides a sort of lever which can be used to produce or to prevent the occurrence of the effect. The point (is) that causes must be potentially levers—even if in practice often unpullable ones. (3:127)

Prudence as Thought and Action: Hobbesian Prudence

Natural Relation and the World for Action

A theory of action makes necessary a "natural relation," rather than a "philosophical relation" to the world for action, which is the world of exteriority. Hobbes was quite clear that insofar as "the knowledge of consequence"—or Science—was only that of a philosophical relation, science could not know well enough for action.

> No man can know by Discourse, that this, or that, is, has been, or will be; which is to know absolutely; but only that if this be, That is; if this has been, That has been; if This shall be, That shall be; which is to know conditionally; and that not the consequence of one thing to another; but of one name of a Thing, to another name of the same Thing. (1:50)

The "natural relation," fusing cause and agency, where things are brought about by causes, rather than one thing being observed to be followed by another, introduces into action "the actual power and efficacy which causes do have." (3:129) The natural relation to the world for action has room for the interests of the human agent of action. The "philosophical relation," on the other hand, is the world of the spectator, and "In this spectator's world there seems to be no room for the interests of agents." (3:138) Moreover, the natural relation to the world for action has room for the ordinary experience of the actor. The room for ordinary experience is the space to experience one's circumstances as a power of causality—the present means to obtain some future apparent Good. It is also the space for the experience of a knowing, a prudential knowing. What is this knowing that is experienced as the knowing of ordinary experience? It is the knowing built up by the psychology of association regarding the connection between events that arises out of the experience of acting with "designe."

But the psychology of association can only build a knowledge based on past experiences. Hobbes did not make an experienced connection between things past a necessary connection between things to come. Since the future was "but a fiction of the mind" (1:21) the relation of prudence to the future was left by Hobbes as one of expectations. The function of prudence for the agent of action was to minimize the failure of expectations. Deliberation was concerned with the internal states of the agent of potential action.

The World as Hobbesian Spectacle

Hobbes has so juxtaposed prudence in relation to the world for action that this world was made by Hobbes to be both spectacle and non-spectacle. It was made non-spectacle because the Hobbesian actor entered into it as part of the search for the causes of the actor's own fortune, causes both of good fortune and of evil fortune. It is spectacle because the world as events is known through observation as antecedence and consequence. Contiguity in time may be observed, but the true causes or the necessary connections between antecedence and consequence may not be known. Nevertheless, there is an assurance or certainty of belief on the part of the Hobbesian actor "that there be causes of all things that have arrived hitherto, or shall arrive hereafter." (1:82) An assured belief in pure causality is an assured belief in the world as pure spectacle. A "pure spectator" in search of pure causality understands the world as pure spectacle. (2:219) Pure spectacle is the world for action without either good or evil. The pure thought of science might seek to confront the world as pure spectacle, but what dominates the actions of the Hobbesian actor is always "regulated thought", or thought regulated by "some desire and designe" of the actor's.

Possessory Certitude and the World for Action

Hobbes imprisoned prudence in the never ending dilemma of separating out the evil that may be "functioning of 'things' themselves" from the evil that is brought into "a functioning of thought which bears on things." (2:219) The world for action is always an object of knowledge, just as it is always a pattern of events into which the actor enters as part of "some desire and designe".

For Hobbes, there was no "right reason" of prudence, such as Aristotle had posited. (4:206) There was only ceaseless endeavor to secure one's self against feared evils and to procure for one's self a desired good. The curiosity of men was directed to "the search of the causes of their own good and evill fortune." (1:82) Desire and aversion are given material form through deliberation. In Hobbes, deliberation is likened to seeing, a seeing by which the sequels of action, and the foresight of what ensues as consequence for desire and aversion, becomes good or evil.

> . . . ; the good or evill effect thereof dependeth on the foresight of a large chain of consequences, of which very seldome any man is able to see to the end. But for so farre as a man seeth, if the Good in those consequences be greater than the Evill, the whole chaine is that which Writers call *Apparent*, or *Seeming Good*. And contrarily, when the *Evill* exceedeth the Good, the whole is *Apparent* or *Seeming Evill*. (3:48)

Consequences are defined by Hobbes in terms of a possessory certitude. Possessory certitude is not only the certitude that complements desire, taking the latter in the sense used by Marcel. "Desire refers to something external to myself which I would like to possess." (2:171). Possessory certitude is also a certitude about the world for action that lends itself to a reckoning—to "*addition and substraction.*" (1:33). Reason is nothing but the reckoning of the consequences assigned by thought to the causes and sequels of events—but a reckoning that is always in terms of the fortune specific to the actor.

For the Hobbesian actor, there is no such thing as a "Rationall Appetite." There is only the psychological uncertainty attending the liberty of choice with respect to acting or not acting. This psychological uncertainty is "an alternate succession of Appetites, Aversions, Hopes and Fears." (1:46) Hobbesian deliberation settles the question of volition. Deliberation ends, but it is not constrained to an end. What deliberation ends is the liberty of choice about acting. What ends deliberation is the act of willing. All willed acts are voluntary acts. They are voluntary whether or not they have their source in covetousness, ambition, lust, aversion, fear, hope or despair. Good and evil mean nothing to the Hobbesian actor apart from his own use of them in relation to that which he either desires or dislikes. Action, in terms of normative judgments, involves only the good or evil attending expectations, effects, and instrumental utility. Good and Evil mean nothing absolutely, or in and of themselves, or derivatively, since there is no "Common Rule of Good and Evill, to be taken from the nature of the objects themselves." (1:41)

REFERENCES

1. Hobbes's *Leviathan*—(Rep. of ed. of 1651, Oxford University Press 1909, Imp. of 1929)

2. Marcel, Gabriel—*Presence and Immortality* (M. A. Marcado, Transl., Duquesne U. Press, 1967)

3. Flew, Antony—*Hume's Philosophy of Belief*: A Study of His First Inquiry (Routledge and Kegan, Paul, London 1961)

4. *The Nicomachean Ethics of Aristotle*—(F. H. Peters, Transl., Kegan, Paul, Trench & Co., London 1884)

CHAPTER III

Prudence as Thought and Action: Aristotelian Prudence

Prudence, Sensibilization and Desire

IT IS ARISTOTLE WHO FIXED the concern of prudence onto "matters of practice", or the particulars of action. The capacity for sensation bears a special relationship to the practical. From sensation comes memory. From the sensibilization that is memory comes both prudence and experience. "In men, experience comes into being from memory; for many memories of the same thing result in capacity for one experience." (1:12 Bk. A) The relation of experience to doing something is the relation of knowing the individual thing, but not having "universal knowledge." It is sensibilization that provides the most authoritative knowledge of individual instances, even though the sensations "do not tell us the *why* of the thing." (1:13, Bk. A) It is not that sensations make men know, but that sensations are necessary for knowing. It is this relation of the sensations to the desire for understanding that is, for Aristotle, a sign of the liking by men of sensations. (1:12, Bk. A)

In his review of sensibility, reason and desire as possible grounds of prudence, Aristotle subordinates them to a theory of action. The practical judgment of prudence is a judgment about action, and it encompasses all of the things needed to decide upon the truth of that judgment. Mere sensibility is rejected as absent a capability for action. A theory of action compelled an Aristotelian differentiation between practical reasoning and speculative reasoning. Action cannot be linked to reasoning as such, for "Mere reasoning . . . can never set anything going." Speculative reasoning is rejected, because its separation from desire cuts it off from action. It is only in the conjunction of desire with reason-practical reasoning-that action originates.

Desire, Purpose and Practical Reasoning

It is because of the link with desire that the truth of practical reasoning was not the truth of speculative reasoning. Desire had its own truths. Where desire existed, the function of practical reasoning was to know or apprehend that truth which was "in agreement with right desire." This truth is the truth that emerges from the calculation of means as the way of thinking, for only the "reasoning about means to an end—what may be called practical reasoning"—will generate action. (2:183) Purpose—whether it be "called either a reason that desires, or a desire that reasons"— originates action. The conclusion of Aristotle was that purpose "is the cause—not the final but the efficient cause or origin—of action." Purpose itself had its origin in "desire and calculation of means." (2:183) Desire, because it was not a faculty of reason, invested purpose with what reason could not. The calculations of reason invested purpose with the truth to which it must assent. Desire invested purpose with the rightness of that which must be pursued as its object.

Purpose becomes action originating. Purpose, then, as part of a theory of action, must include a theory of the person as action originator. Both reasoning and desire are introduced, as synergistic elements of purpose, into a theory of action in order to explain the origination of action. Reasoning, in the two modes of "affirmation and negation" (or assent and denial) conjoins with desire, in its two corresponding modes of "pursuit and avoidance" (or attraction and repulsion). (2:182) The constituents of purpose lie in this correspondence between the two modes of reasoning and the two modes of desire. "This faculty of originating action constitutes a man," wrote Aristotle. (2:183) How is it that reason desires and desire reasons? The explanation of Aristotle is that

> . . . purpose necessarily implies on the one hand the faculty of reason and its exercise, and on the other hand a certain moral character or state of the desires; for right action and the contrary kind of action are alike impossible without both reasoning and moral character." (2:183)

The Thatness *and* Whatness *of Prudence*

There was no prudence without a calculative or deliberative way of thinking. The calculative was denominated a division of the rational by Aristotle; but not all calculation or deliberation was prudential reasoning. For Aristotle, it was a question of both the thatness of prudence and the whatness of prudence. The *thatness* of prudence was identified as the human capability of originating action through purpose. The *whatness* of prudence was the knowing which ensued from a way of thinking by a something which cognizes. The Cartesian *res cogitans* was always present as the originator of every act of prudence.

In terms of its *whatness*, prudence was not a knowing of sensory data. It was not identical with inquiry. The correctness of its knowing was not to be tested by the norms of either science or opinion. It was neither sagacity nor "happy guessing." Prudence was a factual knowing "in the domain of practice" at the level of abstraction at which one perceived by apprehending, but without the demonstrative proof of scientific knowing. So in its *whatness*, prudence was neither guessing nor sagacity, because calculation was not necessary for either of these. Prudence was not science, because to know scientifically is to know free of error. Prudence was not opinion, because opinion is a settled knowing that leaves no room for deliberation. Prudence is not identical with inquiry, but it rests on deliberative knowing as "a particular kind of inquiry." (2:195)

There could be no prudence without deliberation, and no deliberation without calculation; but not all calculation leads to "good deliberation," however impossible good deliberation may be without calculation. In his summation of good deliberation, Aristotle wrote:

> So good deliberation simply (or without any qualifying epithet) is that which leads to right conclusions as to the means to the end simply; a particular kind of good deliberation is that which leads to right conclusions as to the means to a particular kind of end. And so, when we say that prudent men must deliberate well, good deliberation in this case will be correctness in judging what is expedient to a particular end of which prudence has a true conception. (2:197-98)

Non-Possessory Certitude and Prudence

Aristotle, unlike Hobbes, had made prudence a way of thinking that also directed the acting human to another type of certitude. The prudence of Aristotle had not assigned the world for action to pure exteriority. Aristotelian action involved a "seeing" by the actor that was not just sensory cognizing. Experience had a place in Aristotelian prudential foresight, not because it could supply a demonstrated proof about what action to take, but because experience gave to persons "a faculty of vision which enables them to see correctly." (2:201) Aristotelian "seeing" is grounded in intuitive reason. The "seeing" of intuitive reason is intuitive perception, an apprehending of "the unalterable first principles," or that which is anterior to demonstrated knowing and to the factical particularity of "practical calculations". (2:200) Intuitive reason apprehends that which is "the source of our conception of the final cause or end of man." (2:200) This pre-cognitive apprehending by intuitive reason is the presencing virtue that constrains the sensory cognition of prudence from becoming only a detached and detachable cleverness in calculating.

Aristotelian prudence, while not excluding the "possessed certitude," opens the way for the inclusion of another type of certitude in prudential thinking. The second type of certitude is what has been termed by Marcel "the existential certitude." Comparing the two types of certitudes, Marcel has noted:

> By essence, the possessed certitude can be passed on or transmitted. It does not cling to the one who comes by it . . .
> Should we not investigate the relation of each of these types of certitude with the one who formulates them on the one hand, and with that on which they bear on the other? Objective certitude tends to depersonalize itself; I am satisfied only on condition that I am able to say: 'It is certain that.' It refers to a structure which I can say is equally that of things or that of ideas. The case of existential certitude is entirely different. Here it is not a question of doing away with the subject but of transforming it." (1:150)

Volition and Prudential Purpose

Prudence was grounded in a theory of action, but action is the outcome of a specific joinder of volition and reason. The analysis of purpose was subsumed by Aristotle under his treatment of *The Will*, where his object was to clarify the understanding of action and to explicate purpose or choice in relation to voluntary action. He was very specific about setting off voluntary acts from involuntary acts, and involuntary acts from acts that were "merely not voluntary." (2:64) A voluntary act is one which originated within the doer, and therefore "originated by the doer"; meaning that the cause of doing the act lies in the doer, who, as the agent of action which he originates, has the volition either to do or not do the act. (2:65)

Volition, however, is wider than choice or purpose. Still, to choose is to will. Purposed acts thus become a special case of voluntary acts. One aspect of their being a special case is that choice or purpose "seems to be," as Aristotle phrased it, "most intimately connected with virtue, and to be a surer test of character than action itself." (2:66) The second aspect of their being a special case is that purposed acts are the object of deliberation.

> The object of deliberation and the object of choice or purpose are the same, except that the latter is already fixed and determined;

when we say, 'this is 'chosen' or 'purposed,' we mean that it has been selected after deliberation. For we always stop in our inquiry how to do a thing when we have traced back the chain of causes to ourselves, and to the commanding part of ourselves; for this is the part that chooses. (2:72)

To say that deliberation constrains volition is to say that a calculative reasoning—the deliberation of a "rational being"—is implied in choice or purpose. Deliberation constrains volition by excluding that which is judged to be impossible, and by excluding that which is judged to be beyond the capability of one's actions, or to be impervious to the effects of one's actions. Matters of necessity and the eternal invariables of nature are excluded from deliberation. Exact knowledge leaves no space for deliberation.

For Aristotle, it was the presence of control and of uncertainty that provided space for deliberation. Deliberation is appropriate when control is possible and when uncertainty enters into general rules of action. Control introduces "reason and human agency" as a cause of change. What humans can effect by their being originating agents of action is the matter appropriate for deliberation, as these effects are then controllable matters of conduct. Since man "originates his acts," action is a power with respect to whatever thing may be placed within the ambit of that power.

As for a choice or purpose, it was defined by Aristotle "as deliberate desire for something in our power." (2:72) Desire was made congruent with the outcome of deliberation about the power to do through action. " . . . if the purpose is to be all it should be, both the calculation or reasoning must be true and the desire right, and that the very same things must be assented to by the former and pursued by the latter." (2:182). This deliberation is a deliberation about means, rather than about ends. "We desire in accordance with deliberation," wrote Aristotle (2:72), for otherwise means would not be those voluntary acts by which both the virtue of the actor and the power of originated action are disclosed.

Virtue, Volition, Reason and Prudence

Aristotle establishes a ground for a congruence in action between ends and means. That is, he removes the enigma from his explanation that reason desires and desire reasons. Still, is there a difference between ends and means? If so, what is the significance of this difference for prudence? The Aristotelian analysis of action involves an interplay of three categories—virtue (the moral), reason (the intellectual), and originating power (the will).

Prudence is not just a capability for action in matters of practice—a practical reasoning about means to an end, as distinct from speculative reasoning. It is also a capability "that apprehends truth by reasoning or calculation, and issues in action in the domain of human good and ill." (2:187) It is this spilling out of action into the realm of good and ill that makes critical for prudence "a certain moral character or state of the desires." (2:183) The Aristotelian difference between ends and means, therefore, is this:

> . . . The rightness of the purpose is secured by (moral) virtue, but to decide what is proper to be done in order to carry out the purpose belongs not to (moral) virtue, but to another faculty. (2:204)

What is this human power or faculty, and what is its relevance to prudence? What Aristotle has reference to is something that bears on prudence, but is by itself nonprudential. The Aristotelian reference is to a nonprudential form of the calculative, namely, cleverness, or "The power of hitting upon and carrying out the means which tend to any proposed end." (2:204) Cleverness separates means from "moral virtue". Cleverness is, in other words, indifferent to the virtue of any end and, therefore, indifferent to whomever is the actor. Base or noble end, prudent or villain as the actor, the stance of cleverness is that the rightness of the purpose of either is a matter of indifference. Both prudent and villain can be clever about the means for the attainment of their ends. Nevertheless, for the prudent, Aristotle imposed something more as essential.

> Now, this power (cleverness) is not identical with prudence, but is its necessary condition. But this power, the 'eye of the soul' as we may call it, does not attain its perfect development (as prudence) without moral virtue, as we said before. (2:204)

For prudence to emerge beyond the mere cleverness of the calculative, the essence of the matter is that virtue be comprehended as a ground of thinking. rather than as something to be learned apart from reason itself. Virtue is not a reference norm external to thinking prudentially. That would leave prudence as a way of thinking without moral virtue. Virtue would then be solely an analytic derivative, a by-product of cognition, a learned aspect of social character formation. Aristotle, who concluded that virtue became manifest in prudential thinking, put the matter in terms of his difference with Socrates about it.

> Virtue is not simply a formed habit *in accordance with* right reason, but a formed habit *implying* right reason. (The reason of the acting agent.) But right reason in these matters is prudence.
>
> So whereas Socrates held that the (moral) virtues are forms of reason (for he held that these are all modes of knowledge), we hold that they imply reason." (2:206. Italics in original)

Prudence, then, is itself a presencing virtue, a virtue that presents itself in reason, and by its presence as prudence, "the single virtue of prudence implies the presence of all the moral virtues." (2:207)

Aristotle made prudence the ruling virtue—but ruling in the interests of wisdom. The wisdom to be attained through prudence was that power of human reason to unite both the intuitive and the demonstrative of knowing, and thereby to attain, through wisdom, knowledge of "other things of a far diviner nature than man." (2:191). By his judgment of the superiority of wisdom over prudence, Aristotle cast doubt on whether, of all things in the universe, man is the best of all.

REFERENCES

1. *Aristotle's Metaphysics*—(Hippocrates G. Apostle, Transl. and Comm., Indiana University Press, 1966)
2. *The Nicomachean Ethics of Aristotle*—(F.H. Peters Transl., Kegan Paul, Trench & Co., London, 1884)
3. Marcel, Gabriel—*Presence and Immorality* (M.A. Marcado, Transl. Duquesne University Press 1967)

CHAPTER IV

Prudence as Other-Than-Action

1.
SENSIBILIZATION, IMAGINATION AND THOUGHT

PRUDENCE AS ACTION YIELDS MORE READILY to explanation than does prudence as other-than-action. It is easier to visualize how action effects a conjunction with materiality than does other-than-action. Once a conjunction is effected, the fundament for explanation is supplied by materiality.

In their relation to prudence, other-than-action and action are not opposites. Nor is the other-than-action of prudence identical with prudence as non-action. Neither action nor non-action are free of the motive causes of action. It is right here—because of this motive effected conjunction with materiality—that the fundament for explanation is supplied by materiality. An explanation of action grounded in materiality requires a causally linked regulative mechanism of some order of complexity by which to explain a sequence of action.

The other-than-action of prudence brings to the fore the *that* of the prudential which might not be regulated by the motive causes of action. What, then, is the conjunction effected with materiality by the other-than-action of prudence? It is assumed that the explanatory capacity of materiality is not exhausted by an explanation of prudence as action. But what does that explanatory capacity field as an explanation of the other-than-action of prudence?

Imagination: Hobbesian

The imagic and imagination provide a first entry into the other-than-action of the prudential. Neither Hobbesian nor Aristotelian actors can do without an imagic. Nor can either do without imagination. Yet imagination for the Hobbesian actor is not the same as imagination for the Aristotelian actor. Their respective explanations of imagination each involve an imagic. They differ, however, in their explanations of the imagic as part of the other-than-action of prudence.

For the Hobbesian actor, the image of an object is not the imagic equivalent of the object itself. It cannot be, since all the sensible qualities are in the object, and not in the subject who perceives, or by other sensibilities, obtains an image of the object. There can only be an image—which is no more than a "fancy" or appearance of "externall things." (1:12) Moreover, whatever it is that appears as an imagic to the senses of the Hobbesian prudent is subject to sensory decay over time. "Imagination therefore is nothing but *decaying sense*." (1:13)

All this must be understood in the context of a present that is always a sensory present. It is in time, that the sensory present is changed into the sensory past. The imagic appears as a succession of sensory images, each corresponding to an event in time. The imagic is that "originall fancy" of an external thing which was once presently apparent to the senses, but which is no longer in the sensory present. All images decay in time in relation to other presently sensed images. Decay is a matter of sensible dominance. Images of the sensory past no longer predominate in the senses, but fade into the obscurity of weakening impressions. "From whence it followeth, that the longer the time is, after the sight, or Sense of any object, the weaker is the Imagination." (1:14)

The imagic as the content of imagination limits the Hobbesian actor to imagining only that which was once sensibly apparent to him as an image. That is to say, nothing can be represented except that which was once presented. It is by virtue of this limitation that the imagination is transformed into memory of past sensory appearances. "Much memory, or memory of many things, is called *Experience*." (1:14)

The Hobbesian prudent is left with every appearance a relative appearance. No imagic presentation yields any knowledge about the truth of that which appears as having sensible qualities. As to this position, Aristotle put it that one must say "not that an appearance just exists, but that an appearance exists *for him* to whom it appears, and *when* it appears, and *in the respect* in which it appears, and *in the manner* in which it appears." (2:69 BkΓ)

The other-than-action of prudence, then, fixes the content of that which is sensorily there to be acted upon by a Hobbesian actor. Nothing can be an object of imagination that was not formerly existant as a present sensory object. How it is perceived or imagined as a sensory existant is also a matter of its location in a sensory sequence. The succession of things in present sensation is the succession in which they continue as past sensations. The coherence of the latter is established by the coherence of the former.

> But because in sense, to one and the same thing perceived, sometimes one thing, sometimes another succeedeth, it comes to passe in time, that in the Imagining of any thing, there is no certainty what we shall Imagine next; Only this is certain, it shall be something that succeeded the same before, at one time or another. (1:19)

Thought: Hobbesian

All this, however, takes place outside of thought, nor does it regulate thought. Sensibility and the imagining of the things that formerly were sensible existants are but part of the other-than-action of prudence. Still another part is thought. The world as it appears to the Hobbesian actor is without a regulated order of succession. But the world as an object of thought to the Hobbesian actor is one that is an object of regulated thought. The world as a succession of imagined sensible existants is without certainty. But the succession of thoughts brought to bear on the world are absent this infirmity. Mind has a capacity for an orderliness that the world of sensible existants does not. "When a man thinketh on anything whatsoever, his next thought after, is not altogether so casuall as it seems to be. Not every thought to every thought succeeds indifferently." (1:18-19)

It is the "Trayne of Thoughts" that leads to the essence of the other-than-action of prudence for the Hobbesian actor. For what is then introduced as yet another part of this other-than-action is Hobbesian "designe." The Hobbesian linkage is between desire and designe. When compared with the Aristotelian linkage, the difference is that there the linkage is between desire and reason. Hobbesian calculation presupposes a kind of self-conscious understanding on the part of an actor.

Hobbesian understanding is what is "raysed" in a person by imagination. Imagination follows the "reliques" of the sense; that is, it follows the signs and symbols of sensibility. The understanding of the Hobbesian actor includes both an understanding of his own volition and an understanding of his conceptions and thoughts. "Mentall Discourse" is the "Trayne of Thoughts" within the ambit of the understanding, which, in turn, is grounded in the sensible fundament of imagination. (1:18)

Thought is regulated by the conjunction of desire with designe. Desire, as part of the other-than-action, controls action through its regulation of thought. Desire evokes calculative thoughts. These are thoughts of the means by which to attain that which is the aim of desire. The aim of present desire is always a future something. But present desire cannot escape two present necessities. One necessity is that of finding a present power of action. The beginning of action, for the Hobbesian actor, is always "some beginning within our own power." (1:20) The other necessity is present imagining of the power of desire realized as possible future actions. Present desire as possessory desire necessarily imagines possible future actions as the realization of a possessory future.

All possessory desire, however, is limited by the finiteness of sensory based imagination itself. Neither idea, nor conception, nor image, nor time, nor power, nor force can be imagined in other than finite terms. Imagination dips into, but does not encompass the ends and bounds of the imaginable. Desire must therefore collapse into "designe." It is the regulated thought of designe that relates action as a present power to the non-existent future as the imagined existence of a future present. The explanation of action is thereby subordinated to designe. In turn, designe is transformed into the strategy of action. Strategy is designe technologized into the regulative dominion of action in time so as to pre-empt a possessory future.

Enmattered Thought

Imagining is made of sensibilization. With the Hobbesian actor, sensibilization is used to unite imagination with thought. The effect is to equate thought with a representation. The Hobbesian actor is sensibilized by the sensible qualities of the objects that are imagined as an appearance or a representation. Sensibilized thought is the material relation of the Hobbesian actor to the object that materializes as a sensory representation. Because it is sensibilized by the qualities of external objects (the Hobbesian "cause of sense" (1:11)), Hobbesian thought is but the receptive side of sensibilization. Because it is sensibilized, the Hobbesian imagination is without a formative power, requiring always a prior sensory image. It is, moreoever, without duration, existing only as a "decaying sense." (1:13)

Hobbesian thought is always limited by the content of its representations. The sensibilized thought of a Hobbesian character, and therefore the prudence of a Hobbesian actor, is enmeshed in sensory appearances. It is enmattered thought. Still, these sensibilized appearances are as much intimations of something as they are representations of something; a "seeming, or fancy" of "sense matter without," to use the Hobbesian phraseology. (1:11) In short, they are not determinative representations. Nor are the representations of Hobbesian thought of an architectonic nature; they are not system creating. The empirics of being sensibilized are such that external things appear in time in either object entirety or in their object partiality, and in neither case is there an established order of succession as between appearances.

The enmattered thought that is Hobbesian in character cannot make conceptually determinate knowledge about the world external to the actor. Thought involves a representation, but what that representation is as knowledge is left indeterminate. The interest in knowing of the Hobbesian actor, however, is not basically epistemological. The enmattered thought or "Mentall Discourse" that is Hobbesian in character is frustratingly inconclusive about the very thing that is of central concern to the Hobbesian actor; namely, "absolute knowledge of Fact, past, or to come." (1:49) In enmattered thought, fact originates as sense and becomes memory.

> No man can know by Discourse, that This, or That, is, has been, or will be: which is to know absolutely but only, That if This be, That is; if This has been, That has been; if This shall be, That shall be: which is to know conditionally; . . . (1:50)

Rather than an interest in knowing that is epistemological, the basic interest of the Hobbesian actor is the desire to know the possibility of an event in relation to action, or the possibility of action in relation to an event. The foresight that is prudence lies in "conjecture" about experience with these action/event or event/action relationships. Prudence has to do with the expectations of the actor that emerge from such conjecture. The more prudent the actor, the less seldom is it that his expectations will fail him. "And though it be called Prudence, when the Event answereth our Expectation; yet in its own nature, it is but Presumption." (1:21) Prudence is not the foresight of things to come (for prudence does not supply the will by which they are to come), but it is experience with the signs of antecedent/consequent or consequent/antecedent "whereby to guesse at the Future time." (1:22)

Here again, imagination is not a formative power with respect to knowledge of the world in which, and as to which, actions are taken. The Hobbesian imagination is a formative power only with respect to desire and "designe" on the part of an actor. Here it is not the decaying images of sense to which the Hobbesian imagination has reference. Rather, the reference is to the imagining by the actor of what can be done with anything whatsoever when that actor so has it as to be able to produce effects with it by his actions. (1:20) Here it is that prudence and expectations can intersect.

The Hobbesian imagination infuses the actor with a particular being-in-the-world without providing him with any determinative knowledge of the world. The Hobbesian imagination that is a formative power fixes the actor into a relation between the events that he desires and his possible actions. The Hobbesian actor is always brought back to his power as an agent of action with possessory desire and "designe," and it is this that regulates enmattered thought, guiding it into the thinking that directs all thoughts in the way to attain what the Hobbesian actor would have. (1:20)

Aristotelian Sensibilization

What does the person subject of sensibilization bring to knowledge of the world and to being-in-the-world? That which is central to the matter of the other-than-action of prudence is enveloped within this question. It is the question that is posited in the treatment of the relation of imagination to thought. The treatment by Hobbes is in contrast with that by Aristotle. Hobbes, too, is at variance with Heidegger, who also delves into the relation between the two. The latter begins his inquiry into thinking by positing a situation in which a person stands face-to-face before a tree. "What becomes of the face-to-face, the meeting, the seeing, the forming of the idea, in which the tree presents itself and the man comes to stand face-to-face with the tree?" (3:42) It is a situation that is reminiscent of the Aristotelian position, namely:

In general, if indeed only what is sensible exists, nothing would exist if things with a soul did not exist, for then there would be no power of sensation. For one thing, it is equally true that the sensibles and the effects of the sensibles would not exist (for the latter are affections of that which senses), but for another, it is impossible that the underlying subjects which cause the sensations should not exist, even if there is no sensation of them. For a sensation is surely not a sensation of itself, but there is also something else besides that sensation which must be prior to the sensation; . . . (2:68)

Aristotelian thought is not the enmattered thought of the Hobbesian actor. Yet a capability for sensibilization is an attribute of the Aristotelian actor. This attribute of the Aristotelian actor, however, is not the exclusively receptive sensibility that characterizes the being sensibilized of the Hobbesian actor. The Hobbesian subject of sensibility is one who is sensibilized. The Aristotelian subject of sensibility is one who engages in sensibilization. Sentient beings are beings capable of sensibilization, and to the extent that objects are the objects of sense, images may be produced by actual sensations. But sensibilization is not sensation bound.

Imagination: Aristotelian

The Aristotelian imagination as sensibilization is the faculty by which an image presents itself to one for purposes of coming to judgment about something. The judgment that attends imagination is not the persuasive judgment of reasoned conviction. It is possible in the case of the Aristotelian imagination to have "false imaginings concerning things of which we hold at the same time a true conception." (4:127) Sensible objects may be presented to sentient beings as actual representations, or as perceptions of special attributes, or as perceptions of common attributes of a class of things. Things which have magnitude appear as sensibles. As "sensible magnitudes" they seem to have an existence independent of the subject. In relation to the subject who sensiblilizes, sensation is the "form" taken by sensibles; the form "given" to them in sensibilization. "Imagination, however, is distinct from affirmation and negation, for it needs a combination of notions to constitute truth or falsehood." (4:145)

Thought: Aristotelian

Aristotelian thought contrasts with the enmattered thought of the Hobbesian actor. The thought of the latter is unable to separate things from their matter. The thought of the latter is also unable to make mind become an object of thought to itself, because the subject, as a sensibilized subject, cannot think except as it is acted upon. Aristotelian thought is the exercise of an intellectual capacity to think and to conceptualize. Intellect, "being in its essential nature an activity," (4:135) is not just that which is acted upon. It is capable of separating things from their matter. (4:133) It is also capable of including

> mind itself . . . among the objects which can be thought. For where the objects are immaterial that which thinks and that which is thought are identical. Speculative knowledge and its object are identical . . . Mind is the power of becoming such objects without their matter; whereas the mind will have the attribute of being its own object. (4:135)

Moreover, the enmattered thought of the Hobbesian actor confines him to the "actual knowledge (that) is identical with the thing known." But Aristotelian thought recognizes the "potential knowledge (that) is prior in time in the individual." (4:139)

The Aristotelian treatment of sensibilization results in the vesting of the imagination with far more than a power of object representation. The imagic includes more than the representation of sensible form. There is an "imagination of sense" (4:155) which supplies objects with a material form, and to which present sensations can be referred in order to match object with sensation. These are not, however, the images for thinking. There is a particular way in which Aristotle relates sensibilization to thinking. Thought is not enmattered, but it is not thereby emancipated from sensation. The imagic of thought consists of mental images—the "intelligible forms of things." " . . . Mental images are like present sensations, except that they are immaterial." (4:145) They are extracted, as it were, from their locus in the sensible forms of the things that exist independently of the actor as "sensible magnitudes." Hence the Aristotelian position that: "without sensation a man would not learn or understand anything, so at the very time when he is actually thinking, he must have an image before him." (4:145)

Imagination and Action: Deliberative Imagination

A form of representational imagination becomes part of the other-than-action of prudence because of its relation to thought. The Aristotelian imagination also becomes part of the other-than-action of prudence because of its relation to the motivation to act. There is a kind of imagination that can provide a motivational cause for action. It was identified by Aristotle as "deliberative imagination." (4:155) How is it that non-material images have a motivational power such that they can move one to act? Mental images serve as present sensations of that which, in its material form as an object of sensation, has already become an object of thought. The realm of sensibility does more than just present the actor with the objects of sense. The more is that "in the region of sense the objects of pursuit and avoidance have been defined" for thought. (4:143) Thought, with mental images serving as present sensations, pursues and avoids what sensation has already affirmed as pleasant or painful for the actor.

Given a sensibly grounded motivation in which the objects of pursuit and avoidance have been defined for thought, "deliberative imagination" involves the influence of images on the calculative as an aspect of the other-than-action of prudence. With deliberative imagination "you calculate as though you had the objects before your eyes and deliberate about the future in the light of the present." (4:143) Motivation becomes a conjoining of imagination and desire with acts directed to an end. Imagination is then likened by Aristotle to a kind of "intelligence, if we regard imagination as one species of thinking." (4:151) Imagination, as a motivational contributor to action, is restricted in its relevance to the practicalities of acting. "By intelligence we mean that which calculates the means to an end, that is, the practical intellect." (4:151)

Thought and Imagination: Hobbesian and Aristotelian

On the face of it, the equivalent of the Aristotelian "deliberative imagination" is the Hobbesian sagacity of "designe" regulated thought. In both, the imagination functions as a motivational contributor to action, imagination joining with the optative to provide present sensations through images. In both, thought is the practical thought that starts from the object of desire or appetancy. In both, the end of this regulated train of thought is some apparent but situationally limited "practical good." In both, the possibility of an experience is the possibility of action in relation to an event, or the possiblility of an event in relation to the actions of an agent of action.

On the face of it, however, all that is established is that both the Aristotelian actor and the Hobbesian actor possess a practical intelligence, and that thereby both can act with reference to "that which calculates the means to an end, that is, the practical in intellect." (4:151) It has already been noted that what is central to the matter of the other-than-action of prudence is enveloped within the following question: What does the person subject of sensibilization bring to knowledge of the world and to being-in-the-world?

All that the Hobbesian actor brings to the world is the calculative knowledge of the practical intellect. Volition is reduced to the mechanisms of sensible materiality. The imagination that is the decaying sense of enmattered thought is only an empirical imagination. It is not the mental images of the intelligible forms by which things are separated from their matter—which is the transcendent imagination of the Aristotelian actor. It confines the world within the limits of perception, excluding the world as an object of ideas of the mind. Thinking by the Hobbesian actor involves assumptive analysis, analysis of assumptions about the external reality that is presented to the actor as appearances. The speculative intellect is denigrated as an unguided "Trayne of thoughts." There is a sensibilized subject who acts as an agent of action. There is, however, no "underlying subject" with a distinctive "being" or substance. (2:108 Bk Z) There is, in fact, no "substance of anything" for the Hobbesian actor. (2:68 BkΓ)

REFERENCES

1. *Hobbes's Leviathan*—(Rep. of ed. of 1651, Oxford University Press 1909, Imp. of 1929)
2. *Aristotle's Metaphysics*—(Hippocrates G. Apostle, Transl. and Comm., Indiana University Press 1966)
3. Heidegger, Martin *What Is Called Thinking?*—(Harper & Row 1968 ed.)
4. Aristotle *De Anima*—(R.D. Hicks, Transl. and notes, Cambridge University Press 1907)

CHAPTER V

Prudence as Other-Than-Action

2.
DELIBERATION AND INWARDNESS: THE HOBBESIAN PRUDENT

Designe

IN THE THOUGHT of the Hobbesian actor "designe" is antecedent to deliberation. It is in "designe" that there lies that fundament with respect to the future by which the future is made to be the possessive future of an acting agent of action.

"Designe" is the resultant of imagination and a kind of perception that is essentially inward in its seeing. "Designe" involves the perspicacity of prudence about purpose-serving events. That prudential perspicacity is either how, in purpose-serving events, "a multitude of things" conduce to a "designe," or to what "designe" they may be conduced and brought to serve. (1:55)

Hobbesian prudence, no matter how perspicacious it may make the Hobbesian actor about "designe," is nevertheless separated from action. "Designe" prepares the way for action. It does not settle the matter of acting, or not acting, pursuant to "designe." The bridge from "designe" to action is supplied by deliberation.

> When in the mind of man, Appetites and Aversions, Hopes and Fears, concerning one and the same thing, arise alternately; and div-

ers good and evil consequences of the doing, or omitting the thing propounded, come successively into our thoughts; so that sometimes we have an Appetite to it; sometimes an Aversion to it; sometimes an Aversion from it; sometimes Hope to be able to do it; sometimes Despaire, or Feare to attempt it; the whole summe of Desires, Aversions, Hopes and Fears, continued till the thing be either done, or thought impossible, is what we call Deliberation. (1:46)

Desire Itself

The deliberation of the Hobbesian prudent is not focused on ends. There is no interplay of ends and means in Hobbesian deliberation. "Designe" is not the equivalent of end in the thought of the Hobbesian actor. Not only is there no "ultimate ayme" or end, but there is no place in that thought for ends. Whether classified as immediate or ultimate, the ends of action are not objects of desire. What is intelligible desire for the Hobbesian actor is an unbroken line of successes.

> *Continuall success* in obtaining those things which a man from time to time desireth, that is to say, continuall prospering, is that men call FELICITY; I mean the Felicity of this life. (1:48)

It is not only a possessive future, but also a possessive past that is at stake for the Hobbesian actor. Possessiveness is a Hobbesian stance that carries both backwards and forwards in time. The object of desire is desire itself. Desire itself is extended in time. Desire itself transcends the time of the sensory present. Desire itself abides. It abides in the agent of action, transcending the time and object of any present desire. It abides in the agent of action as part of a learning whereby the attained desire of time past is used as the way to progress to still another object of desire in future time. Desire itself as the object of desire moves action, and inclinations to action, towards the assurance of future desires. Desire itself, while not leading either to any particular or to any ultimate end, does lead to a desire for that power by which to realize desire itself. It does so because the Hobbesian actor "cannot assure the power and means to live well, which he hath present, without the acquisition of more." (1:75) That "restlesse desire of power after power" is the desire always to order the present for a better advantage in obtaining the desires of a future time. The positioning of desire itself in time characterizes the possessiveness of time as a state of desire in the Hobbesian stance.

> For there is no such thing as perpetuall Tranquillity of mind, while we live here; because Life itselfe is but Motion, and can never be without Desire, nor without Feare, no more than without Sense. (1:48)

Inwardness

Deliberation, like designe, is another domain of inwardness. Designe is inward in its seeing. Deliberation involves the inwardness that is the non-visible origins of visible actions. Deliberation is that whereby, in the mind of the agent of action, a terminus is put both to volitional irresolution and to volitional non-resolution.

> Every *Deliberation* is then sayd to End, when that whereof they Deliberate, is either done, or thought impossible; because till then wee retain the liberty of doing, or omitting, according to our Appetite or Aversion. (1:46)

The inwardness of the seeing of Designe is that in purpose-serving events the Hobbesian actor has revealed to himself that for which he has Appetite or Desire and that towards which he has Aversion. His Being-In-The-World is then manifested through characterization of it in terms of objects of desire or objects of aversion. What is Good is that for which the Hobbesian actor has desire. What is "Evill" is that which is an object of aversion. These normative characterizations — Good and Evill — are person contingent and psychological in essence. "There being nothing simply and absolutely so; nor any common Rule of Good and Evil to be taken from the nature of the objects themselves; but from the person of the man . . ." (1:41)

Moreover the inwardness of the seeing of "Designe" is also linked to imagination. Although designe is derived from the sensory experience of purpose-serving events—with prudence as the equivalent of much experience—designe also presupposes subsequent events that have not yet taken place. Designe, in short, imagines a future. Since it is an imagined future, thought about "whither, which way, and what" necessarily precedes action. (1:39)

The Passions

But thought about the future, for the Hobbesian actor, begins with the passions: "Appetite, Desire, Love, Aversion, Hate, Joy, and Griefe." (1:42) These inward passions are the small invisible beginnings of the thought that culminates in visible actions. They are accompanied by internal, psychological states of feeling about the objects of the world.

> *Pleasure*, therefore, (or *Delight*) is the appearance, or sense of Good; and *Molestation* or *Displeasure*, the appearance, or sense of Evil. And consequently all Appetite, Desire, and Love, is accompanied with some Delight more or lesse; and all Hatred, and Aversion, with more or lesse Displeasure and offence. (1:42)

The passions bring the Hobbesian actor to that final inwardness—Liberty. Both Appetite and Aversion involve a liberty to do, or not to do, according to what the passion of each is in an actor. Neither Appetite nor Aversion involve the rational as a constraint on volition. There is only the liberty of an actor to do or not do in accordance with what each as Appetite or Aversion is within him. Liberty is a matter of volition, "For a *Voluntary Act* is that which proceedeth from the *Will*, and no other." (1:47) The liberty of an actor to do or not do according to the passion within him involves an alternating succession of the various passions. It is here that there lies the source of volitional irresolution. Deliberation terminates the underlying, but irresolute liberty. Volition thereby becomes *"the last Appetite (or Aversion) in Deliberating."* (1:47) Willing becomes an act of deliberation.

It is not reason, but "Designe" that is regulative of thought. "For the thoughts, are to the Desires, as Scouts, and Spies, to range abroad, and find the way to the things desired." (1:57) Desire and Designe contain and guide thought, directing it to the attainment of what desire would have. Designe fixes the "Discourse of the Mind" on the seeking or hunting out of the relation of effect to cause and cause to effect, until the thought chain of means comes to a beginning that is within the power of the actor. Desire and Aversion speak imperatively to the actor, but deliberation speaks subjunctively, linking supposition to their consequences; "as, *If this be done, then this will follow*; and differs not from the language of Reasoning, save that Reasoning is in generall words; but Deliberation for the most part is of Particulars." (1:47)

The Felicity Driven Actor

It is not the chain of means—which may also be regarded as a chain of consequences—that is the object of regulated thought. Desire and designe regulate thought in order to attain the constitutive substance of what is desired. The imagined chain of consequences that attend a deliberated sequel of actions are part of a future imagined as a possessive future. In deliberation about a future so imagined, the Appetites and Aversions of the Hobbesian actor transform that future into a foresight of desired good and aversive evil. This foresight of the passions is the calculation of the Hobbesian actor. All possessive futures are futures so calculated. In the transcendent time of desire itself, they become part of that continuum of "continuall prospering," a continuum made up of "continuall success," which is Felicity.

The past is neither readily nor totally disposable in Hobbesian deliberation. First of all, the Hobbesian actor is a Felicity driven agent of action. Felicity contains the past as a presence of desire. The past as desire is there as desire attained. But the past is not there as desire whose progress is assured. The Felicity driven actor, the actor driven by desire itself, desires that the way of future desires be assured. Past desire is both prelude and more than prelude to future desires. As more than prelude, past desire is there as present means for the attainment of the next desire in time. As merely prelude, by itself it is there only as an unassured present power and means for the enjoyment of present desires. The ground for its assurance lies in further acquisition. In either case, the past persists as a time transcending presence of desire.

Past and Future In Deliberation

While the Hobbesian future is necessarily an imagined future, the past nevertheless enters into the imagination of the future. The imagined future is not the presumptive future of prudential thought. The presumptive future of prudence is a represented future—that is, a future presumed from a past representation: "As Prudence is a *praesumption* of the *Future*, contracted from the *Experience* of time Past." (1:22)

There is the imagination that is the "decaying sense" of sensory representation. It is the progressively obscure after-image of what has been seen. The post-perceptual sensory impression becomes less vivid and fades with time and place changes in the body of the perceiver. It is in comparison with "other objects more present, succeeding and working on us, (that) the Imagination of the past is obscured and made weak." (1:14) But this is the past as memory.

More important for the imagination is the past as experiences of sensory appearances. Then the past enters into the imagination by fixing and constraining the pattern of imaging sensory phenomena.

> But as wee have no Imagination, where of we have not formerly had Sense, in whole, or in parts; so we have no Transition from one Imagination to another, whereof we never had the like before in our Senses . . . But because in sense, to one and the same thing perceived, sometimes one thing, some times another succeedeth, it comes to

passe in time that in the Imagining of anything, there is no certainty what we shall Imagine next. Onely this is certain, it shall be something that succeeded the same before, at one time or another. (1:19)

The Practical Imagination

There is also, however, the imagination that is not the imagining of sensory phenomena. It is "when imagining anything whatsoever, we seek all the possible effects that can by it be produced; that is to say, we imagine what we can do with it, when we have it." (1:20) This is the imagination of regulated thought; the thought that is governed by designe. The imagination of regulated thought is the practical imagination. The practical imagination is an empirical aspect of regulated thought. It is the practical side of what Heidegger has identified as "pure imagination." In Heidegger's analysis, the "primordial act of thinking is an act of pure imagination." (2:158) The imagination of primordial thinking is thought that envisions something, "an envisioning which is at once a forming and a projecting." (2:158) Thought that is regulated by desire and designe is thinking that is constitutive of a future reality which is also a possessive future. The practical imagination envisions a possessive future by acts of representation that are formative or productive in their essentiality. Except for the practical imagination, the Hobbesian treatment of imagination leaves it without any formative power. In all other respects the imagination is an aspect of sensation. It is then only a sensibilized imagination, rather than a pre-materialization that is formative of a possessive future.

Prudence, designe or practical imagination, and deliberation are tied together. Hobbesian prudence is the judgment brought to bear on purpose—serving events. It is a judging of either how they may be fitted to a designe, or how a designe in hand may be fitted to the events. The inwardness that is the practical imagination of designe is the privateness of its envisioning. Prudence is the discipline imposed on the practical imagination by experience and memory. Hobbesian deliberation is deliberation about whether to do or not to do the thing which the practical imagination has projected and made formative as an imagined future.

REFERENCES

1. *Hobbes's Leviathan*—(Rep. of ed. of 1651, Oxford University Press 1909, Imp. of 1929)
2. Heidegger, Martin—*Kant and the Problem of Metaphysics*—(Churchill, James S., Transl., Indiana University Press 1962)

CHAPTER VI

Prudence as Other-Than-Action

3.
DELIBERATION AND INWARDNESS: THE ARISTOTELIAN PRUDENT

As BETWEEN ARISTOTELIAN AND HOBBESIAN PRUDENTS, the difference between the deliberation of the one and the deliberation of the other is that the logical materialism of the Hobbesian falls away before the prudence of the Aristotelian. At the threshhold of deliberation the Aristotelian prudent disposes of three questions. The questions are those the answers to which are essential to him as an actor. The first of these is the relation of virtue to prudence.

Prudence, Deliberation and Purpose

The Aristotelian union of virtue with prudence puts another face on deliberation. The union of the two is contained in the all inclusive statement by Aristotle: "The presence of the single virtue of prudence implies the presence of all the moral virtues." (1:207) The union of virtue with prudence must appear in the relation of deliberation to purpose. The connection between virtue and purpose was, for Aristotle, more intimate than that between virtue and action. (1:66)

Choosing is willing, but not all willing is choice or purpose. Acts purposed are voluntary, but not all voluntary acts are deliberately purposed. Purpose is not wish, for the embrace of wish includes the impossible, while the embrace of purpose includes only that which the actor thinks possible by his own agency. Nor is purpose opinion, for choice requires the rightness of cognitive knowledge. What is distinctive about choice or purpose is that "it implies calculation and reasoning," which provide it with the ground of its preference. (1:68) The process of calculation and reasoning is deliberation. Aristotle put it that

> ... the things that we deliberate about are matters of conduct that are within our control ... for besides nature and necessity and chance, the only remaining cause of change is reason and human agency in general. Though we must add that men severally deliberate about what they can themselves do. (1:69)

Purpose is that which is chosen after deliberation. The agent of action "originates his acts"; he acts "for the sake of something else"; and what he deliberates about is what he can himself do. So, for prudence, there is always a matter of practical action in which there is sought "some end, in the sense of some realizable good." (1:192)

Deliberation is always inquiry. For the Aristotelian prudent, however, it is not about the ends to which the inquiry of deliberation is directed. Deliberative inquiry is directed to means. The Aristotelian reference to examples is solely to an actor who is a member of a profession, and who therefore has the end of his profession settled in his mind, and who seeks on each occasion the means whereby to attain some particular end through his own agency. The "something else" that is not a particular end of action is a settled matter not subject to deliberation.

Aristotelian prudence is quite clear that "In practical matters the end is not a mere speculative knowledge of what is to be done, but rather the doing of it." (1:356) Yet that aptness to act, by the exercise of which one can become a prudent actor, requires an actor who wills and acts that are willed. The Hobbesian naturalism about deliberation falls away before the Aristotelian prudent. Will, for the Hobbesian actor, is the final act of determination, an act resulting from an iterative and sequential mechanism of appetitive choice, one that puts an end to deliberation. For the Aristotelian actor, however, will is more than the bare mechanism of arriving at a decision about doing or not doing that terminates deliberation.

No act of the Aristotelian prudent can be willed, the cause of which does not so lie within the agent of action that he has the discretion to do or not to do. Willed acts are voluntary acts, including choice of acts in the situation of a given alternative. Although what is then chosen to do would not otherwise be done, "The choice of the particular thing that is done is voluntary." (1:61) Willed acts involve a "state of the agent's mind at the time" of action. It is this state of mind that makes voluntary acts willed acts. "They are desired or chosen at the time when they are done, and the end or motive of an act is that which is in view at the time." (1:59)

There is a duality in the position taken by Aristotelian prudence about an actor who acts "through ignorance." Ignorance about what? "The sphere of action is that which is alterable." (1:187) It is alterable because of the particularities of action that characterize the acts of prudence. It is ignorance, then, "of the particular occasion and circumstances of the act," specifically

> They are—first, the doer; secondly, the deed; and thirdly, the circumstance or occasion of it; and sometimes also that wherewith (e.g., the instrument with which) it is done, and that for the sake of which it is done (e.g., for protection), and the way in which it is done (e.g., gently or violently). (1:63)

What about another kind of ignorance—not of particulars, but "ignorance of the universal"? (1:63) By the "universal," Aristotelian prudence means "ignorance of the principles which should determine preference." This ignorance is more than judgmental error, for it goes beyond the choice of means for the realization of an end. It is the ignorance that constitutes vice, and it lies outside of Aristotelian prudence.

The Relation of Virtue to Vice

It is vice, the relationship of which to virtue and prudence is the second threshold question to be disposed of by the Aristotelian prudent. Vice is what "makes men unjust and bad generally." It is the ignorance of the "vicious man" about what ought and what ought not to be done. (1:63) The stance of Aristotelian prudence is unequivocally "that it is impossible to be prudent without being morally good." (1:205)

Now the notion of virtue is not foreign to Hobbesian prudence, but Hobbesian virtue is another matter. To the Hobbesian, intellectual virtue is an acquired capability or "Wit" that is experientially developed by use of two sensory attributes. "This NATURALL WIT, consisteth principally in two things; *Celerity of Imagining*, (that is, swift succession of one thought to another;) and *steddy direction* to some approved end." (3:53) This is the Wit that underlies the designe of prudence. Nor is the idea that a person may possess a special fitness foreign to Hobbesian prudence, but it is constrained to the "Worthiness" of "*Aptitude*," or the functionally useful qualities associated with "a particular power, or ability." (3:74) The "seeing" of Hobbesian prudence is restricted to the foresight of expected outcomes or "good and evill consequences, and sequals of the action whereof we Deliberate." (3:48)

The virtue of Aristotelian prudence infuses "a certain complexion to our idea of the end" of action. What issues forth as voluntary action is the performance of acts which themselves conduce to and sustain the originating power of virtue in the actor. (1:79) The permeation of virtue into "determining the end" still leaves the actor with the prudential obligation of choosing particular acts. It is in this sense that while the end is optative, the actor must yet "deliberate and choose the means thereto," (1:74) and through deliberation guide desire to that which is within the power of the actor. This is the desire reasoning and the reason desiring that is the essence of the calculation of Aristotelian prudence. It is, in short, the analytical or technical aspect of prudential deliberation. Vice is not prudence. In the language of Aristotle, "vice perverts us and causes us to err about the principles of action." (1:205) Vice obliterates the pre-emptively regulative principles that are not only the originating source of action, but also the "ends for the sake of which acts are done." (1:188) Vice leaves the origination and the choice of acts without principle.

Virtue, Prudence and Deliberation

Mere differential preference as between actors is not a prudential preference of virtue over vice. What is essential for the Aristotelian prudent is not just to establish an inseparable junction between virtue and prudence. It is also essential for the Aristotelian prudent to establish an inseparable junction between prudence, reason and calculation. The latter junction is a necessity of purpose. The deliberation that precedes purpose involves the practical reasoning by which action is originated through the regulation both of the modes of calculation and the modes (pursuit and avoidance) of desire.

> Purpose, then, is the cause—not the final but the efficient cause or origin—of action, and the origin of purpose is desire and calculation of means; so that purpose necessarily implies on the one hand the faculty of reason and its exercise, and on the other hand a certain moral character or state of the desires; for right action and the contrary kind of action are alike impossible without both reasoning and moral character. (1:183)

Deliberation and calculation are one in Aristotelian prudence. For purpose to be what "it should be" in its guidance of action, both the reasoning of calculation must be true and rightness attach to desire. The cognition of prudence is not the demonstrative knowledge of science. Aristotle concluded that prudence "cannot be a science because the sphere of action is that which is alterable." (1:187) It is because of this dependence on an underlying variability of causes that prudence lies outside of demonstrative knowledge. Prudence deals with a human good in which there is implied an advantage to the actor. It does not exclude the actor "deliberating well about what is good or expedient for himself." (1:186) There is always a realizable good which practice can take as an end. Deliberation seeks "to arrive at what is best for man in matters of practice." (1:192) Practice especially is the realm of factual particularities. Here, too, it is in the domain of practice that the doing or not doing of acts is the object of prudential directives.

The deliberation of Aristotelian prudence, reduced to its simplest terms, is "correctness in judging what is expedient to a particular end, of which prudence has a true conception." (1:198) While Hobbesian prudence distinguishes between prudence and craft, Aristotelian prudence distinguishes between prudence and cleverness. These are not parallel distinctions. The craft that is set off from Hobbesian prudence is a perversion of it.

> To Prudence, if you adde the use of unjust, or dishonest means, such as usually are prompted to men by Feare, or Want; you have that Crooked Wisdom, which is called CRAFT. (3:56)

The cleverness that is differentiated from Aristotelian prudence "is its necessary condition." (1:204) It is that power of a person which, though independent of moral virtue, is "the power of hitting upon and carrying out the means which tend to any proposed end." (1:204) Depending upon whether the end be virtuous or base, both an actor as prudent and an actor as villain can exercise cleverness. "To decide what is proper to be done in order to carry out the purpose belongs not to (moral) virtue, but to another faculty." (1:204) Cleverness, that is to say, is a form of the calculative, but the calculative does not invariably proceed by reasoning deductively from "the good" as a major premise or principle of action. Nevertheless, as an indispensable part of prudence, cleverness helps to explain why it is that prudence "makes us adopt the right means to the end." (1:207)

Still, that is not all there is to the significance of cleverness. Its calculative utility for any purposive activity, emancipated as it is from the moral ends of prudential virtue, also emancipates the practical reasoning of the calculative by freeing it from being exclusively focused on means—ends relationships. Through cleverness, which Aristotle characterized as "the eye of the soul," practical reason is also freed to deal with the effectiveness of any action in any dimension of preference. The performance that was set down by Aristotle as the end of a practical science is a realm more inclusive than the domain of prudential practice.

Hobbesian prudence rejected "right reason," which for the Aristotelian prudent, meant "in accordance with prudence." (1:206) But in that rejection Hobbesian prudence also discarded all linkages between virtue and prudence. The logical naturalism of Hobbesian prudence leads it to a rejection of any possibility of an order of things being implicit in prudence. For Aristotelian prudence on the other hand, what is present in "the single virtue of prudence" as an "excellence" of man's nature is the possibility of an order of things.

Virtue, Prudence and "The Good"

The third question for the Aristotelian prudent has to do with the ethicality of prudential action.

Where is the goodness or virtue of action if there is deliberation only over means? There is one branch of thought, to be found in *The Metaphysics*, in which the notion of "good" becomes entwined in the Aristotelian "principles." After reviewing the several senses or meanings of the concept of "a principle", Aristotle arrives at the common characteristic of all principles, namely, that they are "the first from which a thing either exists or is generated or is known." This summation of his thought about principles is reinforced by a list of examples: "Therefore, nature is a principle, and so is an element, and also *thought* and *choice*, and a *substance* and a final cause; for the good or the noble is a principle of the knowledge and of the motion of many things." (2:73-74 Bk Δ)

The Aristotelian "final cause" places the context of a certain logical naturalism about the "good" in human thoughts and actions.

> . . . the final cause is an end, and as such it does not exist for the sake of something else but others exist for its sake. Thus if there is to be such one which is last, the process will not be infinite; but if there is no such, there will be no final cause. But those who introduce an infinite series are unaware of the fact that they are eliminating the nature of the good, although no one would try to anything if he did not intend to come to a limit. Nor would there be intellect in the world; for at any rate, he who has an intellect always *acts* for the sake of something, and this is a limit, for the end is a limit. (2:37, Bka)

At this point, the notion of "good" is without ethical content. It is there as an outcome of logical analysis in the metaphysics about final cause. There would then be no difference between "the good" and "the apparent good" as denotive terms. So concludes Aristotle in disposing of final cause: It "is a cause in the sense that it is the end or the good of the others; for that for the sake of which the others exist or are done tends to be the best or their end. Let there be no difference here between calling this 'the good' or 'the apparent good'." (2:75, Bk Δ)

A specifically ethical content to the notion of "good" is introduced by the treatment of motive as final cause. There it is that virtue is associated with the notion of "good." The Aristotelian explanation for this is:

> . . . in matters of conduct the motive (end or final cause) is the principle (beginning or efficient cause) of action, holding the same place here that the hypotheses do in mathematics . . . ; it is not reason but virtue, either natural or acquired by training, that teaches us to hold right opinions about the principle of action. (1:234)

A difference between "the good" and "the apparent good" then takes on significance. The desirable of the optative (what is striven for in action), if it is "the good" that is intended, but "the bad" ensues, then it was not the end object. If it is what is "apparently good" that is intended, then it is the outcome of this seeming good that was the end object. Only half the answer to these discrepant outcomes is given in Aristotle's statement, "As neither of these alternatives quite satisfies us, perhaps we had better say that the good is the real object of wish (without any qualifying epithet), but that what seems good is the object of wish to each man." (1:73)

Were this all that was stated, it would have to be concluded that the Aristotelian prudent is without a preemptive regulator of choice, even though, for Aristotle, prudence and moral virtue were inseparably joined to one another. (1:341)

The Aristotelian resolution of the question of indifference to "the good" goes to the quiddity of the actor. The starting notion is that "the good is the real object of wish." It is the notion that the ideal is the reality of the optative. The difference between actors is the difference between them in the optative reality of each as an originator of their respective acts.

> . . . the good man, then, wishes for the real object of wish; but what the bad man wishes for may be anything whatever; . . . for the goods or ideal man judges each case correctly, and in each case what is true seems true to him.
> . . . I think there is nothing so distinctive of the good or ideal man as the power he has of discerning these special forms in each case, being himself, as it were, their standard and measure. (1:73-74)

It is now possible to understand what it is about the logical naturalism of Hobbesian prudence that falls away before Aristotelian prudence. What falls away has to do with the actor himself. In Hobbesian prudence the actor has the attributes of sensibility, but he lacks the quiddity or Being of the actor who is an Aristotelian prudent.

Reciprocal Subjectivity and Subjectivity Itself

Hobbesian prudence and Aristotelian prudence must be differentiated in a fundamental aspect of each. The comparison is between Hobbesian designe and Aristotelian virtue. Hobbesian designe is the subjectivity of the agent of action that is the converse of the objectification of the world for action. It is reciprocal subjectivity. The complete sensibilization of both actor and the world for action, whereby the actor is himself completely reduced to attributes of sensible materialization, of necessity excludes everything other than reciprocal subjectivity. Felicity is the only real object of wish of reciprocal subjectivity, given Hobbesian designe what it is. For Aristotelian virtue, however, "The function of the practical intellect is the apprehension of truth in agreement with right desire." (1:183)

Aristotelian virtue is the subjectivity itself of "moral character." It enters into the world for action through sensibilization. Sensations are liked, not only "for their own sake," but also because, as it was put in *The Metaphysics*, sensations make for knowing and "all men by nature desire understanding." (2:12 Bk A) The virtue that is subjectivity itself—non reciprocal subjectivity—enters into prudent action, but in the case of Aristotelian prudence "for the possession of the virtues knowledge is of little or no avail." (1:41) The Aristotelian requirements for acts in which virtue is manifest are that

> . . . in the case of the virtues, a man . . . must also be in a certain state of mind when he does it; i.e., first of all, he must know what he is doing, secondly, he must choose it, and choose it for itself; and, thirdly, his act must be the expression of a formed and stable character. (1:41)

All acts, whether those of Aristotelian or Hobbesian prudence, originate in subjectivity. The actor, as person, "originates his acts." (1:71) The power of a person lies in this origination of acts. "This faculty of originating action constitutes man." (1:183) A compulsory act is such that the external cause of it leaves nothing to be contributed by the actor. (1:162) The sensibilization of the actor and the world for action in Hobbesian prudence supports the contention that the appearance of good is not within the control of the actor. As desiring responds to appearance, it is in what appears that there is an apparent end. Nature, so to speak, by deciding what is presented as appearance also fixes an apparent end for each actor. The Hobbesian prudent, who functions in the context of reciprocal subjectivity—where the subjectivity of the actor is a reciprocal of the sensibilized objectification of the world for action—desires an apparent good. He must decide, nevertheless, from what is externally presented to him as the sensibilized appearance of things.

The possessory stance of the Hobbesian actor has its fundament in reciprocal subjectivity. (3:41) Whatever it is by way of appearance that nature decides for Hobbesian sensibilization, subjectivity has a space still for its own determination of a particular "good." Nature presents the "countenance" of promise to the Hobbesian actor. Sensibilization has "apparent signes (which) promiseth Good." (3:41) In Hobbesian prudence there is either the "good" so promised, or the utilitarian "Good" of means, or the "good in Effect, as the end desired." The latter gives rise to the pleasures of "Expectation, that proceeds from foresight of the end, or consequence of things." (3:42)

Aristotelian prudence rejects the contention that nature decides appearance. The rejection is on grounds of subjectivity itself. The actor, as person, always contributes something himself. There is some thing more than just the "countenance" of promise that nature presents to sensibilization. "If, I answer," wrote Aristotle, "each man be in some way be responsible for his habits or character, then in some way he must be responsible for this appearance also." (1:78) It is from subjectivity itself that there originates an end which, by being truer than a particularized end of choice, functions as a pre-emptive regulator of chosen ends.

> . . . the striving towards the true end does not depend on our own choice, but a man must be born with a gift of sight, so to speak, if he is to discriminate rightly and to choose what is really good; and he is truly well-born who is by nature richly endowed with this gift; for, as it is the greatest and the fairest gift, which we cannot acquire or learn from another, but must keep all our lives first as nature gave it to us, to be well and nobly born in this respect is to be well-born in the truest and completest sense. (1:78)

Prudence, Deliberation and Dialectics

In Aristotelian prudence deliberation is identified with inquiry. Granting that "inquiry is not always deliberation—mathematical inquiry, for instance, is not—deliberation is always inquiry." (1:71) At the same time, prudential deliberation is infused with uncertainty.

> Matters of deliberation, then, are matters in which there are rules that generally hold good, but in which there is an element of uncertainty. In important matters we call in advisers, distrusting our own powers of judgment. (1:70)

Finally, Aristotelian prudence, not being the demonstrative truths of speculative reason, involves inquiry that is not the inquiry associated with science.

In sum, the deliberation of prudence has a dual aspect. One aspect is inquiry itself. The other aspect is relationship, the relationship that has its origins in the element of uncertainty. Aristotelian prudence seems to all but by-pass the relationship in favor of inquiry. Hobbesian prudence, on the other hand, seems to all but by-pass inquiry in favor of relationship. Yet there is a relevant mode of Aristotelian inquiry that involves relationship. It is the Aristotelian dialectic. As inquiry, the dialectic is a search for the essence of that which is being inquired into. As procedure, it involves others in a relationship of inquiring.

> The way to the 'what is' consists in a sequence of questions and answers; in the search for the definition philosophers join forces and pool resources. In exceptional instances the dialectician may ask for, and receive, an account from himself, yet the primal form remains that of a quest undertaken in partnership with others. (4:50)

The scope of the dialectic was enlarged by Aristotle to include more than definition. He made its scope "broad enough to accommodate a great variety of questions, including those of popular interest." (4:56) The separation that ensued, because of this enlargement of scope, between dialectic and philosophy brought dialectic to a position such "that Aristotle himself, when he defines dialectical syllogisms as making use of opinions, contrasts these opinions with the 'true' and self-evident propositions that are used by science." (4:66) As to these matters that were the subject of prudence, Aristotle did not advocate an absolute precision of reasoning. Prudence has its own kind of inquiry in deliberation, and no more should be required, wrote Aristotle, than that "in each kind of inquiry, just so much exactness as the subject admits of." (1:4)

As inquiry, then, dialectic becomes a scrutinizing method with only "so much precision" and no more. In any event, precise enough to know what actions to take, starting from the foundation of what is known to the actor.

> Aristotle's reason for saying that precision beyond a certain degree is not to be expected in ethics is that (a) any general account is bound to obscure the variations in obligation that arise from the varieties of circumstances attending the performance of any action, while (b) the particular account will have to be so hedged with qualifications if it is to fit the particular case (as the general account does not), that it will inevitably lack the simplicity which Aristotle regards as characteristic of precision. This does not mean that there is not in each set of circumstances a right answer to the question of how one should act. (5:86-7)

In Hobbesian prudence every shred of the tie between dialectic and philosophy has disappeared. What remains is the structure of a relationship that is neither dialectical nor disputatious. It is "Counsell". Hobbesian deliberation includes "Counsell" because the latter has been set apart from command. The imperative that is command needs only volition of the actor, "and the proper object of every mans will is some Good to himselfe." (3:195) To give counsel involves a non-imperative relationship. The nature of counsel consists "in a deducing of the benefit, or hurt that may arise to him that is to be Counselled, by the necessary or probable consequences of the action he propoundeth." (3:198) The method of counsel is deductive, for he who counsels "deduceth his reasons from the benefit that arriveth by it to him to whom he saith it." (3:195) The purity of its origin as counsel is the most critical practical concern of the Hobbesian prudent. To be a good counsellor, what is required is that there not be any incompatibility in either ends or interests with those of who is counselled, and that counsel be directed only to the benefit of its recipient. To be an effective counsellor, a number of diverse practical considerations must be taken into account.

REFERENCES

1. *The Nicomachean Ethics of Aristotle*—(F. H. Peters. Transl., Kegan, Paul and Trench, London, 1884).

2. *Aristotle's Metaphysics*—(Hippocrates G. Apostle, Transl. and Comm., Indiana University Press, 1966).

3. *Hobbes's Leviathan*—(Rep. ed. of 1651, Oxford University Press 1909, Imp. of 1929)

4. Solmsen, Friedrich—"Dialectic without the Forms," in Owen, G.E.L., *Aristotle on Dialectic* (Oxford University Press, 1968).

5. Evans, J. D. G., *Aristotle's Concept of Dialectic*—(Cambridge University Press, 1977).

CHAPTER VII

Prudence and Strategies of Thought

WHILE PRUDENCE INVOLVES both thought and action, Hobbesian prudence leads solely to strategies of action. Aristotelian prudence, on the other hand, leads also to strategies of thought. All thought on the part of the Hobbesian prudent is regulated by "designe". Not all thought on the part of the Aristotelian prudent is regulated by "designe". For the Hobbesian prudent, strategies of action require no more than calculations. Strategies of action, for the Aristotelian prudent, involve more than calculation.

The Materiality of Knowing

The physicality of matter enters into the thought of both Hobbesian and Aristotelian prudence. It is enough for the Hobbesian prudent to accept the attributes of matter as providing the material fundament of thought. Thoughts "*singly*, they are everyone a *Representation* or *Apparence* of some quality, or other Accident of a body without us; which is commonly called an *Object*." (1:11) The Hobbesian actor has the immediately sensory knowledge of the representation of an object. It is a knowledge that is attended by the uncertainty that "the object is one thing, the image or fancy is another." (1:12)

What is in point, however, is not just that the Hobbesian actor is confronted by the uncertainty of semblance in the immediacy of representational knowing. There is the further point that the sensibles of the Hobbesian actor are taken to be the equivalence of the motion of matter, of its "many several motions" producing, in turn, the "divers motions" underlying the appearance of "externall things." (1:12) Yet matter is that about which the Hobbesian actor is without any notion, other than that it is the causal repository of sensible qualities.

The Aristotelian prudent puts matter into another context of thought. What is here brought to matter is the notion not that it is not a sensible of materiality, but that it is an empty sensible. "Matter," for the Aristotelian prudent is taken to "mean that which in itself is not stated as being the whatness of something, or a quantity, nor any of the other senses of 'being'." (2:110 Bk) Matter cannot exist simply as a composite of sensory attributes. Matter, as a sensible without its own predicate, is an empty sensible. Sensory attributes "are predicates of a substance, while a substance is a predicate of matter." (2:110 Bk Z)

The Aristotelian prudent opens wide the domain of materiality as the fundament of the regulative mechanism of thought. He does so without excluding the possibility that a train of thought can be regulated—by which one is lead to strategies of action. The Aristotelian prudent also includes within the possibilities of a train of thought that can be regulated—those which lead to strategies of thought. The domain of materiality encompasses substratum and substance as well as matter. These are to be understood as subordinate to "the principles involved in all coming-to-be." (3:345) So understood, all coming-to-be is anterior to sensibles. Change is the modal way in which coming-to-be takes on the appearance of the sensible. However, there is always something that persists through change, that underlies it. What persists is substratum of things.

> It is only substance that comes to be simply; in other cases a thing comes to be this or that. It is evident that there is something underlying change of quantity, quality, etc., since all the categories other than substance involve an underlying substance.

> But the generation even of substance presupposes a substratum; e.g., living things come from seed. Things that come to be come to be by reshaping, accretion, substraction, composition, alteration. But all these presuppose a substratum. (3:345)

Substance is a thing which, in relation to nature, exists as a subject in which, by nature, is incorporated the principle by which it makes itself. In short, it is a subject that has a nature such that it has "an internal principle of change." (3:349) As to man, who is the actor—whether Hobbesian or Aristotelian prudent— "a man, is not nature, but 'by nature'." (3:349) Man is unlike the things that do not exist by nature, for the latter, as things that are made, have the principle of their making outside themselves, or in themselves only *per accidens*. (3:349)

Substance and Sensibles

Matter and substance exist in the chain of coming-to-be. Whether the things of the sensible are generated by nature—or are produced, as that which is generated by art, or by a power, or by thought—they "have matter; for there is a potentiality for each of them to be, and also not to be, and this potentiality is the matter in each." (2:116 Bk) Substance is both the actuality of matter in a particular form and "an underlying subject." The subject is that which underlies the changes of matter. Substance exists among the universe of sensibles in the actuality of its matter, which is the form of the sensible thing. But, as underlying subject, it also exists in the whatness of its essence, or what it is "in virtue of itself." (2:111 Bk Z)

The fundament of things is not just in their being sensibles. A "being" undergirds their appearance to sensibility as the predicates of the actuality of matter. They "have a nature," or a principle of their making as a subject in which nature is. The fundament of "being" in sensibles is a principle of their existence. This principle is both anterior to and independent of the sensibility of perception. Sensibles, in order to be known, must be knowable by

Prudence and Strategies of Thought

more than their representations. There is a knowledge for the Aristotelian prudent which, while not the direct knowledge of the non-empiric eternal forms of platonic reality, is a knowing which "sees" beyond the perceptible properties of sensibles to their more universal coming-to-be and passing-away. (4:72-80) Actuality exists as a reality, but substance and potentiality also exist as the fundament by which reality itself is changed.

The "being" which is by nature established as existence-in-the-world supplies the foundation for more than a possessory stance with respect to the world. Unlike the Aristotelian actor, the "Being-in-the-world" of the Hobbesian actor is always in the modality of a possessory stance. Both time, as the temporally definite event-time of a present strategy of action, and the imagic representation of sensibles, as the knowledge of desire, establish a particular possessory "Being-in-the-world" for the Hobbesian actor. (5) The contrast with the Aristotelian prudent is that the latter is able to reason in terms of strategies of thought with respect to coming-to-be. These strategies of thought are the pre-emptive regulators of the duality of the future. That duality is the future both as an alteration of the present reality of actuality, and also as a change in the reality itself.

Event Time and Psychological Time

In relation to the coming-to-be and passing-away of the Aristotelian prudent, time involves change, but time is not change. "Time is in itself the cause rather of perishing, and only *per acidens* of becoming." (3:391) Change and time are co-perceived. Change (as magnitude) and time are each continuous. While time corresponds to change, however, the latter is in the thing itself. That which is in time, and therefore contained by time, is acted on by time. "Time is not change, therefore, but that in respect of which change is numerable." (3:386) Time and the movement that is change are each the numerical measure of the other.

For the Hobbesian prudent, the present is the conscious "now" of the sensibly present. It is a psychological now. It is a "now" of the acting agent in relation to events that serve to divide time. The Hobbesian actor leaves time "composed of individual nows." (3:416) For him, the "now in so far as the now is a limit, it is not a time but incidental to time." (3:387) Each "now" is a psychologically different time for the Hobbesian actor because of the difference between before and after in 'time'. "There is the same time everywhere at once, but not the same time before and after, because the past and the future change are always different from the present." (3:388) It is the "nows" that are different as between the past and the future, because they do not mark either the beginning or the end of the same time.

The psychological "now" of the Hobbesian prudent is not concerned with the continuousness of time. There is, however, another "now". It is the one holding together past and future as "the link of time". It provides a boundary common to both and establishes the identicality of the limits of the past and future. (3:390)

> The 'now' in the primary sense must be indivisible, and such a now there must be in every period of time. For there is a limit of the past, on this side of which there is nothing of the future, and one of the future, on the far side of which there is nothing of the past; it is, as we maintain, a limit of both. (3:406)

This primary "now" cannot be a divisible interval of time. Otherwise, as the Aristotelian proof goes, it will be a "now" a changing part of which will be past and another part will be future, depending upon how it is divided. Since the primary "now" is then self-identical in both the past and the future, what is to be done through the psychological "now" in the allocation of sensibles in time?

> If one does not treat the moment that divides before and after as belonging to the later time so far as the object is concerned, the same thing will be simultaneously existent and non-existent, and it will be non-existent when it has come into being. The moment is common to the earlier and the later time and is numerically one, but it is not

one in definition, being the end of one and the beginning of the other. But so far as the object is concerned it belongs to the later stage of what occurs to the objects. (3:448-49)

Strategy of Thought

The notion of strategy of thought belongs to the Aristotelian prudent, as against the method of reasoning, which belongs to the Hobbesian prudent. Strategy of thought is not possible unless first, thought is not contained by the imagic representation of sensible perception, and unless second, thought can be emancipated from the regulativeness of desire. In short, eductive representation is a necessity for the Aristotelian prudent. He does not accept that the fundament of thought lies in sensation. It lies in the existence of substance—whatness-essence—the "being" of things which exist in virtue of themselves.

> In general, if indeed only what is sensible exists, nothing would exist if things with a soul did not exist, for then there would be no power of sensation. For one thing, it is equally true that the sensibles and the effects of the sensibles would not exist (for the latter are affections of that which senses), but for another, it is impossible that the underlying subjects which cause the sensations should not exist, even if there is no sensation of them. For a sensation is surely not a sensation of itself, but there is also something else besides that sensation which must be prior to the sensation; for that which moves is by nature prior to that which is moved. (2:68 Bk Γ)

It is not necessary to negate the relation between sensory perception and the representation or appearance of sensibles. Every appearance exists, but it is always "an appearance (that) exists *for him* to whom it appears, and *when* it appears, and *in the respect* in which it appears, and *in the manner* in which it appears." (2:69 Bk Γ) It is necessary to establish that an appearance is not just an imagic representation.

Materiality requires a sequentially linked mechanism by which to explain action. The fundament for explanation, so to speak, is supplied by materiality. Even more to the point, however, the explanation of action in terms of materiality does not exhaust the explanatory capacity of materiality. Sensory based representation, the Aristotelian *phantasia*, establish the preparatory conditions for desire to exist, and the existence of desire is a precondition for action. (6:221-222) Here materiality leads to an explanation of action in essentially physiological terms. Desire, the appetancy which both Aristotelian and Hobbesian prudents recognize as moving the actor to the attainment of a "practical good" through purposive action, is the starting point of action. In the language of the Aristotelian explanation:

> For it is the object of appetancy which causes motion; and the reason why thought causes motion is that the object of appetancy is the starting point of thought. Again, when imagination moves to action, it does not move to action apart from appetancy. Thus there is one single moving cause, the appetitive faculty. (7:151)

What is given is an explanation of action that can be reduced to the physiological, but which in fact exists in the context of connections between representation, desire, and *noesis* or thinking. Both thought and desire require *phantasia*. They so require because both cognition and sensation each have need of their respective objects, although one is immaterial and the other material. Still, it is not necessary that representation be pictorially duplicative. There need only be a " 'what-appears.' " (6:244) The " 'what-appears' " is that which can be comprehended through sensation as a sensible form, and through thought as an intelligible form. (6:145) There is thus a supportable distinction between "a single, isolated impression" (the *phantasia* of appearance) and an educed representation or thought, the appearance of which "is based on experience and reflection" (or *doxa*). (6:245) No understanding without sensation, true enough, but "*thought* either affirms or denies every object of *thought* or intelligible object." (2:70 Bk Γ)

Sensibilization presents images of what appears as objects of present sensation. These are not pictorial representations or duplicative images for thought. Thought, for the Aristotelian prudent "is different from sense-perception." (7:125) What is understood through thought is not the equivalent of what is perceived as a presentation of the senses. Thought does not have the corporeality of sensation. It is, rather, that "Actual perception sets up certain notions (kinesis) in the living creature, which persists in the absence of objects." (6:249) Thought has been separated out from representation. Thought is that by which the actor knows and understands. It includes both the "intelligible objects" of conceptions and the imagic data of sentience. Strategy of thought is possible because mind can think itself, and not just its representations.

REFERENCES

1. *Hobbes's Leviathan*—(Rep. of ed. of 1651, Oxford University Press 1909, Imp. of 1929.)

2. *Aristotle's Metaphysics*—(Hippocrates G. Apostle, Transl. and Comm., Indiana University Press, 1966) For commentary on the use of "being" in Aristotle's writings, see: Buchanan, E., *Aristotle's Theory of Being* (University of Mississippi Press, 1962), Brentano, Frank, *On the Several Senses of Being in Aristotle* (George, R., Trans., University of California Press, 1975).

3. *Aristotle's Physics*—(Ross, W.D. Transl. and Comm. Oxford University Press 1930.)

4. Joachim, Harold H., *Aristotle on Coming-To-Be and Passing-Away*—(Text, Introduction and Commentary) (Oxford University Press 1922); Hintikka, Jaakko, *Time and Necessity: Studies in Aristotle's Theory of Modality* (Oxford University Press 1973).

5. As to "being-in-the world," see Heidegger, Martin, *Being and Time*—(ScM Press, London 1962 ed., Macquarrie, J. and Robinson, E., Transl.) Part One, Division one, II.

6. *Aristotle's De Motu Animalium*—(Text, Interpretation, Commentary, Essays, Nussbaum, Martha C. (Princeton 1978)

7. Aristotle *De Anima*—(Hicks, R.D., Transl., Introductory Notes, Cambridge University Press 1907).

CHAPTER VIII

Being-In-The-World and The Hobbesian Actor

THE HOBBESIAN PRUDENT FUNCTIONS within a chain of material causality. It is a triple chain. There is neither place for, nor necessity for, Being within that chain of material causality. Being is both irrelevant and superfluous for the explanation of either the actions of the Hobbesian prudent, or his reasoning, or his choice of purpose. Each of these is explicable by reference to that triple chain of material causality within which the Hobbesian prudent functions.

The Triple Chain of Material Causality

The first chain of material causality has its basis in relationship. Relationship is a point of union with matter. All relationships, therefore, are evidence of material causality. The second chain of material causality is one that is indigenous to the materiality of sense. Hence it is the chain of a materially sensibilized world for action. The third chain emerges from the possessory stance of the Hobbesian actor towards the world for action.

The Hobbesian actor as a person has his locus in the material chain of relationship. It is there that the concept of the Hobbesian person takes root. The Hobbesian person is an actor. Action and speech are modes of personating. Personating is a peculiarity of relationships between an actor and an other. "To *Personate*, is to *Act*, or *Represent* himselfe to another." (1:123) One can act and speak either in his own name or as the representative of another person. The difference between the two lies in the ownership of the acts performed and the words spoken. The Hobbesian Person may be an actor whose "words and actions (are) *Owned* by those whome they represent." (1:123) Where this is the case, the Hobbesian actor speaks and acts in the context of authority relationships. Authority is "the Right of doing any action." (1:124) The Hobbesian Person, then, is the following: "*A Person, is he, whose words or actions are considered, either as his own, or as representing the words or actions of another man, or of any other thing to whom they are attributed, whether Truly or by Fiction.*" (1:123)

The materiality of sensibilization for the Hobbesian actor is the locus of the second chain of material causality. From birth onwards what the Hobbesian actor has "is nothing else but sense." (1:52) It is this sense from which all thought originates. The Hobbesian actor "can have no thought, representing anything not subject to sense." (1:23) Conception is a conception of something that has first been perceived by sense. Therefore, what is conceived must always have prior determinate place and a determinate magnitude, and its locus and magnitude must have been perceived at a particular time or times. Consequently, for the Hobbesian actor, both "Sense and Memory are but knowledge of Fact, which is a thing past, and irrevocable." (1:36-37) Fact is that to which sensibilization gives place, time, magnitude and duration. Fact involves causality as well as sensibilization.

Sensibilization is the product of the organs of sense, but the causal source of sense is an "Externall Body, or Object" whose qualities for sensibilization are in the objects themselves. (1:11) Sense, then, is "onely Motion, caused by the action of externall objects. (1:41) The mechanics of the motion so caused, however, is paralled by the "divers motions" of the organs "proper to each sense" within the Hobbesian actor, (1:99-12) The direction of the chain of material causality that is in sensibilization is such as to determine—rather than to be determined by—volition.

> For Sense, Memory, Understanding, Reason, and Opinion are not in our power to change; but alwaies, and necessarily such, as the things we see, hear, and consider suggest unto us; and therefore are not effects of our Will, but our Will of them. (1:287)

There is, then, an external material world which has sensible qualities and it impinges on the Hobbesian actor. What emerges from within the latter is a *"seeming, or fancy"* about that external world, which seeming or fancy is termed "sense". It is a world of external materiality that is independent of the actor. The Hobbesian actor wants an explanation of that world in terms of its governing causality. "Anxiety for the future time, disposeth men to inquire into the causes of things." (1:80) So he wants to know from a stance other than one of simple curiosity.

It is the stance from which the Hobbesian actor sets himself to know the world of external materiality that introduces a third chain of material causality within which he exists. The locus of this third chain is in the possessory stance towards the world for action. The hallmarks of the possessory stance are two in number. The first is Felicity, or a "continuall prospering" in desires. (1:48) The second is regulative. It is in this conjunction of the constitutive with the regulative that "the thoughts, are to the Desires, As Scouts and Spies, to range abroad and find the way to the things Desired." (1:57) The possessory stance is defined by this conjunction of the constitutive with the regulative. The possessory stance makes its presence in the Hobbesian actor as a guided "Trayne of Thoughts" that is *"regulated* by some desire, and designe." (1:20)

Differentiation Between Actors

Thus the Hobbesian actor thinks and acts with reference to three chains of causality, each of which has its fundament in materiality. The first is relational, which is a mode of connection/disconnection between actors as material bodies. The second is contingent on the impingement of the world of external objects upon the sense organs of the agent of action. The third is regulative of the thought that precedes action.

It is the third, however, that establishes a base by which to differentiate as between Hobbesian actors. From the starting point of the native faculties with which men are born, the Hobbesian view is that "Nature hath made men . . . equall, in the faculties of body, and mind." (1:94) It is not that Hobbesian equality rules out differences of native faculties as between men. It is that through the employment of these differences men are capable of cancelling out the relative strengths of each other. "The difference between man, and man, is not so considerable, as that one man can thereupon claim to himselfe any benefit to which another may not pretend, as well as he." (1:94)

Nevertheless, it is not in the possibilities for reciprocal negation of differences in native faculties that there lies the greatest equality between men. The greater equality is bestowed by experience. "For Prudence, is but Experience; which equall time, equally bestowes on all men, in those things they equally apply themselves unto." (1:94) Prudence is a capability, an attainable capability." From this equality of ability, ariseth equality of hope in the attaining of our Ends." (1:95)

The Passions, Subjectivity and Materialization

What introduces the differences that are the inequalities between men are the passions. The inequalities between men are the differences between them in their discretion and judgment. The passions introduce differences between men in the "wit" of theirs that is called prudence. What prudence requires is the application of discretion and judgment to "designe" on the part of the actor; and it is a "Wit" that depends much on experience and memory of "like things, and their consequences heretofore." (1:55) The relationship of the passions to prudence is such that "the Passions that most of all cause the differences of Wit, are principally, the more or lesse Desire of Power, of Riches, of Knowledge, and of Honour." (1:56) But the latter, being but "sorts of power," are reducible to "Desire of Power." For the Hobbesian actor, "steadiness" and "quickness of mind" proceed from this desire. It is, in short, productive of attributes that are utilitarian, motivator drivers, and character forming.

The passions both supply a logic as well as fit into a logic of things about action and the Hobbesian actor. The passions supply the basis for a logic whereby actors can be differentiated in terms of qualities essential to the prudence of acts—discretion and judgment. They also fit into a logic about human actors themselves.

Still, what are the passions? The passions are part of the subjectivity of human actors. If this is so, what is that subjectivity of which the passions are a part? Straightforwardly put, for the Hobbesian actor, subjectivity is the interval between two episodes of materialization. Worldhood for the Hobbesian actor consists of episodic materialization. It is episodic in its materialization because he knows neither "naturall causes" nor remote causes, and he restricts himself to perceived "immediate causes" (1:80). He does so because what is perceived as appearance is "Fancy"; because there is only sense to begin with; and because sensible qualities are in the external objects that cause them.

What two episodes of materialization establish the interval of subjectivity? The first episodic materialization is appearance, or Fancy. The second episodic materialization is that possessory materialization of things and effects by which imagination induces "designe," from which proceeds a "Trayne of regulated thoughts." (1:20) That which imagination proposes to "designe," or awakens for it, so to speak, as an object of desire and as the conceivable outcome of action, establishes the pre-materialization of "designe" in subjectivity. Thus is Hobbesian subjectivity no more than the internal reciprocal of objective materialization.

Hobbesian imagination is materialization backwards—from sensory externality to imagic internality. Hobbesian "designe" is materialization forwards—from the internality of imagination to the materialized externality that is the object of desire. The worldhood of possessory stance pre-exists in the subjectivity of the Hobbesian actor as the pre-materialization of that outcome whereby imagination arouses "designe" within the Hobbesian actor.

Time, Desire and Thought

Desire, located as it is, in the interval of subjectivity between episodes of materialization, cannot be disassociated from time. It is this inextricable association between time and desire that is stressed by Descartes, who listed desire as one of the six primitive passions. Generally, the passions bias the actor "to regard much more the future than the present or the past." (2:359) Of desire specifically, and whether in the aversive or the acquisitive mode, Descartes observed that "it is evident that it ever regards the future." (2:359) Desire, as one of the passions, is defined by Descartes as follows:

> The passion of desire is an agitation of the soul caused by the spirits which dispose it to wish for the future the things which it represents to itself as agreeable. Thus, we do not only desire the presence of the absent good, but also the conservation of the present, and further, the absence of evil, both of that which we already have, and of that which we believe we might experience in time to come. (2:369)

Hobbes, like Descartes, had his list of "primitive passions," of which desire is one. But Hobbesian desire is placed in the context of the possessory present, where "we always signifie the Absence of the object" that is desired. (1:40) Desire refers to an imagined materiality whose absence originates the "internal beginning" of a "Voluntary Motion" that can culminate in "visible actions" directed towards its imagined materialization. (1:39) Thus it is that imagination makes the future "but a fiction of the mind" for the Hobbesian actor. (1:21)

While "designe" is the outcome of a possessory imagination, the interval between episodes of materialization that is subjectivity is also the place where there is worked through the essentials of thought, volition and reason in relation to the events expected to follow from action. Thought becomes directed to that which desire and designe would attain. Thought also becomes regulated by the end of desire and designe in its search for productive connections between causes and effects. There, in subjectivity, volition undergoes the ordeal of uncertainty imposed by the intrusion into thought of alternating passions, and by a diversity of promised good and promised evil consequences about that which might be done, should it be done. Deliberation puts an end to this subjective liberty of doing or not doing, culminating as it does in the act of willing with respect to one action or another.

The Reason That Reckons

What about reason? The Hobbesian actor does not begin with reason. He begins with sense only. He begins with a capacity for sensibilization. Reason is something to be "attayned by Industry." (1:36) The prototype of Hobbesian reason lies in its etymology as a term used to denote reckoning or calculation about things.

> The Latines called Accounts of Money *Rationes*, and accounting, *Ratiocinatio*: . . . and thence it seems to proceed, that they extended the word *Ratio*, to the faculty of Reckoning in all other things. (1:29)
>
> When a man *Reasoneth*, he does nothing else but conceive a summe totall, from *Addition* of parcels; or conceive a Remainder, from Substraction of one summe from another: . . . These operations are not incident to Numbers only, but to all manner of things that can be added together, and taken one out of another. (1:32) In summe, in what matter soever there is place for *addition* and *substraction*, there is also place for *Reason*; and where these have no place, there *Reason* has nothing at all to do. (1:33)

What about reasoning by syllogisms and by theorems? Hobbes took up their Greek origins. He characterized the Syllogism as a method of reasoning with speech "which signifieth summing up of the consequences of one saying to another." (1:29) Theorems are a derivative of inquiry into the consequences and producible effects of whatever things an actor may conceive, which is "designe." The Hobbesian actor

> can by words reduce the consequences he finds to genrral Rules, called *Theoremes*, or *Aphorismes*, that is, he can Reason, or reckon, not only in number; but in all other things, whereof one may be added unto, or substracted from another. (1:35)

Where, in the Hobbesian subjectivity that is the interval between episodes of materialization, is the reason that is modes of reckoning? It is preceded by imagination. What distinguishes imagination from the reason that reckons is that imagination functions as the generative or formative capability from which everything else follows. All voluntary action has its "internall beginning" in imagination. Voluntary actions "depend alwayes upon a precedent thought of *whither, which way*, and *what*." (1:39) As for Hobbesian "designe," it, too, has its genesis in the formative capability of imagination. The realm of the pre-calculative lies within the ambit of imagination.

The Future As A Fiction Of The Mind

To assert that the future is a fiction of the mind is to say several things. It is an assertion that prematerialization begins with the pre-calculative. "Designe" imagines. It imagines from a possessory stance. "Designe" imagines a desired not-present or future. As it is a not-present that is located in the interval of subjectivity, it is a future that is not in a mode that impacts on the Hobbesian actor as sensibilization. Moreover, it is a not-present that is not yet the future as a calculated foresight. The passions, too, impart a drive state that is also pre-calculative. What imagination provides is a pre-calculative form of visualization whereby desire might be materialized. The not-present that is the future for the Hobbesian actor is a desired materialization of subjectivity.

"Designe" imagines, but only deliberation commits. It is through deliberation that there is a commitment to either action or non-action. Until then the Hobbesian actor had the liberty of doing or not doing according to "Appetite, or Aversion." (1:46) Deliberation puts a check on the imperatives of subjectivity that have their sources in desire and aversion. Deliberation transforms the imagined not-present or future of "designe" into a not-present of suppositions.

> Deliberation is expressed Subjunctively; which is a speech proper to signifie suppositions, with the consequences; as, *If this be done, then this will follow*; and differs not from the language of Reasoning, save that Reasoning is in generall words; but Deliberation for the most part is of Particulars. (1:47)

The not-present or future of suppositions is the future of calculation. Reason introduces the calculative stage. Reason is thereby used so as to narrow thought to calculation. So narrowed, Reason functions as a subordinated method for clarification of the passions. Not a check, but a clarification. The not-present of supposition is the calculated "foresight" of either "Apparent, or Seeming Good," or "Apparent, or Seeming Evill." Each is comprehended as a relative imbalance of consequences. Each, however, is always comprehended as a desire or an aversion, and hence the calculative remains locked into the alternating sequence of passions. It is always a Reason subordinated to the passion. It is so subordinated because the appetites and aversions that move the Hobbesian actor to voluntary action are linked to the will (to volition), not to Reason. The clarification of the passions is a clarification of the will to act. The actions of the Hobbesian actor may have their beginnings in volition in both "Rationall Appetite" as well as "Covetousness, Ambition, Lust, or other Appetites to the thing propounded." (1:47)

Prudence As Post Calculative Cognition

The calculative that is introduced by reason analytic is not the end stage of calculation. The stage of the pre-calculative, and the stage of the calculative do not, either singly or together, provide sufficient knowledge for prudent action. There is no prudence without the post-calculative. It is prudence that is the post-calculative. The "wit" that is Hobbesian prudence manifests itself as the discretion and judgment by which things in their multitude and in the multitudinous of their appearance are seen either to conduce towards a "designe" or may be brought to yield to one. Prudence is the post-calculative, depending as it does "on much experience, and memory of the like things, and their consequences heretofore." (1:55)

Hobbesian reason, as the analytic of the calculative, is attained by industry, but Hobbesian prudence is attained only by experience. By being so attained, only prudence bridges the past—the present—and the future in experience. It is post-calculative precisely because of the time distributed character of experience. Experience through time brings with it a unity of experience in the consciousness of the actor. The prudence of the Hobbesian actor involves a unity of time-distributed experience with uncertainty. "Signes of prudence are all uncertain; because to observe by experience, and remember all circumstances that may alter the success is impossible." (1:38)

It is experience that determines Hobbesian cognition. It is the cognition that is a derivative of sensibilization. Experience provides the Hobbesian actor with direct, personal, non-mediated knowing. Designe is always absent a corrective. It has always to be realized as an experience to be made possible. The cognition of prudence supplies this missing corrective. Prudence as a post-calculative cognition, through unity in experience of an agent of action that is derived from a time-distributed experience with uncertainty, endeavors to work through to a possible experience for the realization of designe.

As for designe, it is the constitutive side of desire. Designe, unlike desire, is the inward seeing by which imagination pre-materializes the existence of the world from a possessory stance. It is thus that designe is constitutive, while desire is not. Desire is a psychological state. It exists as a state of consciousness in the interval of subjectivity between episodes of materialization.

Hobbesian Being-In-The-World

In subjectivity—Hobbesian subjectivity—the future is pre-materialized. Because it is pre-materialized as designe, the Hobbesian future must necessarily be a fiction of the mind. The future as actuality will consist of episodes of materialization. It is through designe that the Hobbesian actor endeavors to regulate the actualization of the future. The future as designe actualized is a future that is to become materialized through episodes of materialization generated by the agency of his actions. Designe is the "Being-in-the-world" of the Hobbesian actor. (3:93) It is designe that infuses the world for action with a particular existence for the Hobbesian actor. It is designe that gives the environment a non-spatial quality, and from which there intrudes into dealings with entities in the world "certain modes of concern." (3:100) While designe prematerializes, unlike desire, it does not transcend time, for desire continues to exist in the time intervals between episodes of materialization.

The modes of concern that characterize the Being-in-the-world of the Hobbesian actor are all modes of power. Power—Hobbesian power—is consciousness of the variant utility of entities in the world for the materialization of the objects of designe. The concern of power in all its modes and with respect to all entities in the world is the concern of "present means, to obtain some future apparent good." (1:66) The concern of the modes of power is a concern with the relationships by which an actor is united with entities in the world.

The human other is an entity in the world. Being-in-the-world is being in the world with another. The concern of the modes of power include the modes of concern for another. It is a concern with how the attributes and the worth of a person are manifestations of the power of another. That is, a power as a present means to obtain some future apparent good.

> . . . what quality soever maketh a man beloved, or feared of many; or the reputation of such quality is Power; because it is a means to have the assistance, and service of many.
>
> Good successe is Power; because it maketh reputation of Wisdome, or good fortune; which makes men either feare him or rely on him.
>
> The *value*, or Worth of a man, is as of all other things, his Price; that is to say, so much as would be given for the use of his Power; and therefore is not absolute; but a thing dependent on the need and judgment of another.
>
> The manifestation of the Value we set on one another, is that which is commonly called Honouring, and Dishonouring.
>
> To obey, is to Honor; because no man obeyes them, whom they think have no power to help, or hurt them. And consequently to disobey, is to *Dishonour*.
>
> Covetousnesse of great Riches, and ambition of great Honours, are Honourable; as signes of power to obtain them. Covetousnesse, and ambition, of little gaines, or preferments, is Dishonourable.
>
> . . . for Honour consisteth only in the opinion of power. (1:66-68, 71)

The Being-in-the-world of the Hobbesian actor is without both a final end and an idea of the greatest-or-ultimate-good. It is a Being-in-the-world without a teleology that transcends either designe or its acolyte, desire. It is also a Being-in-the-world that is without a point of repose. Every desire realized is but the way to the realization of a further desire. Felicity, as a state in which there can be success in the realization of an endless sequence of desires in time, is the ultimate materialization of the idea of the *summum bonum*. Nevertheless, rooted as it is in a zenoian paradox of an endless present, felicity leaves every future desire without the assurance of its realization as a present actuality.

So it is that the Hobbesian actor gives priority to "a Generall inclination of all mankind, a perpetuall and restlesse desire of Power after power, that ceaseth onely in Death. And the cause of this, . . . because he cannot assure the power and the means to live well, which he hath present, without the acquisition of more." (1:75) It is also a Being-in-the-world with another who is always in competition for power in one or another of its modes. Competitive Being-in-the-world means the way of one Competitor, to the attaining of his desire, is "to kill, subdue, supplant, or repell the other." (1:75) Not surprisingly, therefore, it is a Being-in-the-world in which the practical virtues ("naturall wit") associated with the passions for "the more or lesse Desire of Power, of riches, of Knowledge and of Honour" (all of them modes of power) are held to be preeminent. (1:56)

Finally, it is a Being-in-the-world for the Hobbesian prudent in which there is ignorance on his part both of "remote causes" and of "Naturall causes." This attribution of dual ignorance leads both to credulity and to reliance on the perceptible, sensibilized "causes immediate and Instrumentall." (1:80) Anxiety with respect to the future generates inquiry that can be reduced to knowledge which, in turn, can be employed to gain a present advantage. None the less, anxiety is a condition of Being-in-the-world for the Hobbesian prudent. Cause is omnipresent at all times, but he is without assurance "of the true causes of things, (for the causes of good and evill fortune for the most part are invisible.)" (1:82) The future, generating as it does a psychological condition of "perpetual solicitude" in the Hobbesian prudent, his Being-in-the-world is likened to that of Prometheus.

> For as *Prometheus*, (which interpreted, is, *The Prudent Man*), was bound to the *Caucasus*, a place of large prospect, where, an Eagle feeding on his liver, devoured in the day, as much as was repayred in the night: So that man, which looks too far before him, in the care of future time, hath his heart all the day long, gnawed on by feare of death, poverty, or other calamity; and has no repose, nor pause of his anxiety, but in sleep. (1:82)

In sum, then, the Hobbesian prudent, whose "*Naturall*

vertue" consists of "nothing else but sense" (1:52) has a Being-in-the-world as to which there is neither an order-making regulator within himself, nor an order-originating source in the world external to himself. Because of the first, he exists without Being. Because of the second he exists without a cosmology.

REFERENCES

1. *Hobbes's Leviathan*—(Rep. of ed. of 1651, Oxford University Press 1909, Imp. of 1929).

2. "The Passions of the Soul," in *The Philosophical Works of Descartes*—(E. S. Haldane and G.R.T. Ross, Transl. Vol. I, Cambridge University Press, 1911 Ed. Reprint).

3. Heidegger, Martin, *Being and Time*—(Macquarrie, J. and Robinson, E., Transl., SCM Press Ltd., London 1962).

CHAPTER IX

Being-In-The-World and The Aristotelian Actor

The Three Questions of Materiality

MATERIALITY EXPLAINS MATERIALITY. That which is itself material—the subject—acts with reference to that which is material—the object. The direction of the chain of material causality for the Hobbesian prudent is from the object to the subject. That which is material—the object—impinges on the sensibilized materiality of a subject. The world external to the person exists when and as it becomes an appearance. But the world as it appears to the subject is in need of a corrective before the subject commits himself to becoming an agent of action. The Hobbesian prudent as a subject contains within himself the essential rudiments of capability to deal both with the appearance of the external world and with its corrective adjustments as a prelude to acting. "For besides Sense, and Thoughts, and the Trayne of Thoughts, the mind of man has no other motion." (1:22)

The Hobbesian prudent has addressed himself to answering three fundamental questions. First: How does matter make itself known to other matter? Only by a form of sense, or sensibilization. It is enough "to be born a man, and live by the use of his five senses." (1:22) All other faculties are acquired and enhanced through study, industry, instruction and discipline. Second: How does matter impose itself on other matter; turn it around, so to speak, to one's purposes? Hobbesian designe is that which initiates the endeavor that may culminate in action. Even more than this, designe functions as the prism of imagination through which the external world of appearance is transmuted into a world of desirable outcomes. Hobbesian designe is not constrained to possibilities derived from experience. It is prudence that so constrains it by conceptions of possible experience. Deliberation, by sorting a confusion of the appetitive, constrains designe to intentioned desires. Third: Why does matter impose itself on other matter? Because of the passions, all of which reduce themselves to the power by which to attain a future good through present means, including the power to assure its continued enhancement as power.

Overknowing and Virtue

In all of this, the Hobbesian prudent is careful to avoid two things. These two are overknowing and virtue. As to virtue, the Hobbesian prudent regards it as an empty container. Virtue is absent any linkage to the passions. Virtue is also absent any linkage to cognition. Absent these two linkages, virtue does not fit into a chain of material causality, in consequence of which virtue is out of fit with a possessory stance. One who has no "great passion" for any of the modes of power is without steadiness and direction in his thoughts, and without much judgment, "though he may be so farre a good man, as to be free from giving offence." (1:56,57)

There is no overknowing for the Hobbesian prudent. No overknowing because no order of the world appears except as it may make an appearance in the sensibilized experience of a person. No overknowing, furthermore, because only such pattern of the world is imaginable as has heretofore been included in sensibilized experience. An order of the world to which events can be attributed rests on causes so remote as to be unknowable to the

Hobbesian prudent. His inquisitiveness is not a search for true knowledge, but only a search for whatever causality enters into the good or evil of his own fortunes. Prudence is a corrective knowing, not about an order in the world, but about what pattern design has introduced into the world of events as an order for its own ends. Prudence is a judgment of fit about that pattern.

Underknowing and Overknowing

So materiality explains materiality, but only because materiality has its own gnostics and only insofar as these gnostics allow explanation. The reproach of the Aristotelian prudent to the Hobbesian prudent is that the latter is committed to underknowing. The Aristotelian prudent puts forth a knowing of within and a knowing of without. The Hobbesian prudent takes the position that there can be no knowing of within except from without; that is, from the impingement of the external world on the senses. The Aristotelian prudent queries: Is the knowing of the Hobbesian prudent the only knowing that is knowable to a prudent agent of action? The Aristotelian prudent turns away from the Hobbesian position that without designe there can be no train of regulated thoughts.

Aristotelian prudence recognizes more modes of knowing than does the Hobbesian. The latter rests more on imagination than on rational cognition. Too, where the Hobbesian makes the reason of a prudent actor an acquisition of calculative capability that is attained by industrious application, Aristotelian prudence has its origins in a reason that is pre-calculative. As for matter, Hobbesian prudence—despite its materiality—lacks all concept of matter. It has only an empirics of sensibilization. For Aristotelian prudence, however, the concept of matter is of primary significance, as there is more to matter than its quality of being sensibilized. It is only Aristotelian prudence that is interested in the quiddity or essential nature of the actor himself. So it is that Aristotelian prudence is linked to Being, but not so for Hobbesian prudence. In sum, both the knowing of within and the knowing of without of each prudent will manifest differences, differences that are critical for each and that give the prudence of each its special character. Materiality explains materiality, but what is it of materiality that explains the what of materiality?

Knowing and Materiality

Hobbesian prudence has a formative power with respect to the world external to the actor. Aristotelian prudence has a regulative power with respect to the world internal to the actor. The formative power of the Hobbesian is directly constitutive of the world without. The regulative power of the Aristotelian is derivatively constitutive of the world without. It is only on the surface that the regulative is non-constitutive of the world. It is only on the surface that the formative is non-regulative of the world. Both the world within and the world without are linked through both the formative and the regulative as potencies of an agent of action.

Materiality leads the Aristotelian back to potency; materiality leads the Hobbesian back to power. The presence in the one case, and the absence in the other, of a concept of matter accounts for the difference, which is not just a matter of synonyms. The Aristotelian prudent does not try for any gnostics of matter *qua* matter. The starting point is postulational: "Some matter is sensible and some is intelligible. (2:124, BK.Z) Matter is knowable because "some matter is sensible and some is intelligible." Some matter, that is, can be sensibilized, and in some material things there is that which is purely intellectual or abstractly conceptual. In the latter instance, matter is understood intelligibly, so that a circle of wood is both sensible as wood and, in its circularity, intelligible as a mathematical object. Thus it is that "intelligible matter exists in sensible things but not *qua* sensible, as in the mathematical objects for example." (2:124 BK.Z)

What about the acting agent and the world for action in the *thereness* of its matter as present actuality? An acting prudent is an agent of action. As an agent of action he exists as matter. He also exists as the "underlying subject" of matter. An acting prudent is more than a form in which is incorporated a set of sensibilized attributes of matter. He exists both "as an underlying subject and as matter." (2:138 BK. H) In relation to the former, matter is both a potentiality and the subject which underlies change. An acting prudent, therefore, is the oneness that exists in the form of a person as "potentiality and actuality taken together." (2:145, Bk⊕)

The Aristotelian Potencies

Potentiality is the equivalent of " 'potency,' or 'power' or 'capacity,' or 'capability'." (2:146, Bk ⊕) It is through potency/potentiality that the Aristotelian prudent addresses the question: How does matter impose itself on other matter? Aristotelian potencies are the potency of acting and the potency of being acted upon, each of which illustrates the primary principle of "change in another thing or in the thing itself *qua* other." (2:146 Bk⊕) Inanimate as well as "living things" have their potencies, but those of the former will be without reason while those of the latter "will be with reason." As to these latter potencies, "*knowledge* is reason." The knowledge that establishes the class of "rational potencies" for "living things" (action according to a formula with specifications) involves a deliberate choice of the effects desired. "Thus, everything which is capable according to formula must act on that which it desires, whenever it desires that of which it has the capability and in the manner in which it has that capability." (2:151 Bk⊕)

In the case of the knowledge of practical choice—the practical reasoning that is the formula and specifications which are the potency of performance over whatever matter is to be acted upon—Aristotelian and Hobbesian prudence abut one another. Practical reason—the reasoning of practical choice—is acquired knowledge, an attainment of capability. For each prudent, the capability whose knowledge of performance is reason inclusive, and whose choice of effects is regulated by desire, the action of the agent is for the sake of particular ends—functionally limited action. Nonetheless, while the two prudences may abut one another in the performance of functionally practical acts, their separation is ever sustained by the difference between their respective Being-in-the-World.

The Hobbesian Potencies

Hobbesian potency is not a derivative of reason as an acquired capability. Hobbesian potency is less the knowledge of practical choice than a formative potency. As for that formative potency of the Hobbesian actor, it does not exist in the context of functional action. It does not exist there because by then the world for action has already been materialized in the "Trayne of regulated Thoughts." The formative potency of the Hobbesian actor exists in the conjoining of imagination with designe. It is at this conjunction that the formative potency of pre-materialization of the world comes to be the actuality that infuses the knowledge of action with its potentiality.

For the Hobbesian actor, the imagination is both sense constrained and not sense constrained. It is sense constrained as perception, for then imagination is the recreation of representation. Then, too, no order of the world appears in imagination except as it has appeared in experience; and only that is imaginable which has been experienced as representative. Such is the imagination of "decaying sense," or the succession of displaced representations in time and place. It is the imagination of re-materialization.

That other imagination which is conjoined with designe is the imaginative potency of pre-materialization. Sense alone cannot account for pre-materialization, for the materialization of that which has yet to exist as an actuality. Pre-materialization is not re-materialization. It is not a re-creation of representational materiality. It is a formative potency; a potency that is generated from the actuality of a person as a living thing, and which actuality exists in the person as a being with potency.

Formative Potency

The formative potency of the Hobbesian actor is the imagined production of "possible effects" from the imagined possession of any imagined thing. (1:20) Every possessory order connected with Being-in-the-World is an order of the imagined existence of a being and which proceeds from its existence as an actuality in a person. It is a possessory order which is imagined as capable of existing for that person. The formative potency of the Hobbesian actor is constitutive of an order of Being-in-the-World and regulative of thought within the actor.

Formative potency is the potency whereby to establish an order in the world as an actuality of existence in the world. Formative potency is the ultimate mode of capability whereby matter imposes itself on matter—becomes its potentiality. The formative potency of Hobbesian actors is the potency to establish a possessory order. What is the formative potency of the Aristotelian actor? It may be said that while the Hobbesian actor has a formative potency whereby he acquires a Being-in-the-World, the Aristotelian actor has a formative potency whereby he is invested with a Being-in-the-World. The Aristotelian prudent has also addressed himself to the fundamental question: How does matter make itself known to other matter?

Thought within the Aristotelian actor is also regulated thought, but it is not thought that is regulated exclusively by "Designe." Moreover, the thought of the Aristotelian actor takes matter as knowable in its intelligible as well as its sensible aspects. As for the actor himself, he is not just sense, and therefore only a bundle of sensible attributes of matter, but without an underlying subject. Give the Aristotelian actor as an underlying subject, then sensible attributes become a mode whereby the actuality that is the underlying subject exists throughout the changes by which an underlying subject becomes the potentiality of its matter.

Moreover, with sense attributes there is sensibility, but all sensibility presumes consciousness. All sensibilization, therefore, is sensibilization by a consciousness. Finally, for the Hobbesian prudent, both the matter of things in the world as objects of action, and the matter that is the form of the acting agent are within the same governing principle of all matter—motion (acting and being acted upon). Still, this Hobbesian universal by which matter may come to know matter, is not, for the Aristotelian prudent, an adequate explanation of either the existence of the actor, or of what it is that can be known and generated by that individual form of an acting being in whose substance is both actuality and potentiality. (3:71, 73, Ch. 5)

The Formative Potency of the Aristotelian Prudent

Aristotelian prudence has its own formative potency. It is a potency that is independent of action with designe. It is a potency that knows matter in its intelligible rather than in its sensible aspects. It is a potency in which thought is not regulated by designe. It is a potency that embodies the nonpossessory side of capability. It is a non-calculative potency.

The formative potency of the Aristotelian prudent is the "speculative intellect." The speculative intellect is the capability of mind to reason apart from practical calculations about means for the attainment of a contingent or apparent good. "For the speculative intellect thinks nothing that is practical and makes no assertion about what is to be avoided or pursued." (3:149, Ch. 9) Thus it is a reasoning intellect that is not regulated by any end of desire, so that it is not directed at initiating any action of a functional character.

Formative potency is the potency whereby to establish an order in the world as an actuality of existence in the world. The order in the world that is the potency of the speculative intellect to establish is an order of matter in its intelligible aspects. It therefore stands in contrast to that Hobbesian potency of an order in the world derived from the contingent particularities of sensibilization, and with respect to which imagination conjoined with designe induces a belief in its potentiality as an outcome of action. The Hobbesian potency is a belief that is anterior to reasoning. It is also a belief which looks to the application of acquired knowledge to resolve the uncertainties of that belief. Imagination for the Hobbesian is not thinking. Imagination must be transformed into regulated thought.

The Hobbesian prudent views pre-regulated thought as thinking in a state of drift. It is not thinking, but simply thoughts; a "wild ranging of the (sensibilized) mind." (1:19) Only regulated thought is thinking. It is thinking of a practical kind, directed at the materialization of a possessory order.

The formative potency of the speculative intellect is to materialize a non-possessory order. That it can do so goes back to the Aristotelian position that, unlike sensation, "intellect would seem to be developed in us as a self-existing substance and to be imperishable." (3:33, I, Ch. 4) The activity of intellect is thinking-reasoning, and this activity of thinking is, in itself, a capability. There is a stage in that capability at which "intellect is capable of thinking itself." (3:133, III, Ch. 4)

The formative potency of the speculative intellect is to materialize a non-possessory order. How is it that it can do so? For one thing, it can do so because speculative intellect involves thinking that has been freed of "the imagination of sense," which is the imagination from which designe is generated. Speculative intellect requires a form of the imagic for thinking, but this form involves a "deliberative imagination," or "a form of imagination which comes from inference." (3:155, III, Ch 11) For another thing, the implication of an intellect that is capable of thinking itself is that mind can be its own object of thought, and be self-determining about its operations as thought. The speculative intellect, free to determine itself, is not under necessity to think of the world of being in terms of its sensibilization. There is an inward freedom of the speculative intellect. It is an inward freedom to think about the material world of being in terms of the intelligible aspects of matter—know it in its quiddity by separating it from its matter in the operations of the intellect. (3:133, III, Ch. 4)

The speculative knowledge of a non-possessory order is a knowledge that is separated out from both sensory objects (the intelligible exists in the forms of sensible things) and from action (appetency and the optative). It is not, however, an actual knowledge of "something actually existent." A thing exists in its conceptual abstractness as well as in its material actuality. As concept, a thing exists as an immaterial object that is itself the object of thought by the speculative intellect. "Where the objects are immaterial that which thinks and that which is thought are identical." (3:135, Ch. 14) Through conceptions an ordering of the world of being is possible that escapes the limits of practical thinking about the representations of actual, sensibilized things. Unlike the Hobbesian prudent, who does not view the knowledge of sense as rational cognition, the Aristotelian prudent views both actual knowledge and speculative knowledge as rational modes of the cognitive. In either mode, it is the knowledge of reason "as a self-existing substance."

Virtue, Possessory and Non-Possessory Orders

The possessory and non-possessory orders are orders of Being-in-the-world which stand against one another in human consciousness. The non-possessory order is neither pre-possessory nor post-possessory. The non-possessory order exists in consciousness as knowledge of an order of Being-in-the-World other than that of designe. It stands against a possessory order as a different order. Consciousness knows both sensibilized and non-sensibilized orders of Being-in-the-World.

A possessory order is an optative order. An optative order is one of calculative Being-in-the-World. It is an order of acting and of being acted upon; an order of acting in accordance with formula and specifications, and with choice of acts and ends of action. It is an order in which choice and action are calculated optatively. It is an order in which the actor knows the optative, but not the normative, since the actor knows only the goodness of his own designe. The goodness of a possessory order is only an opportunistic goodness, the good of the optative searching to impose designe on a world of matter that is contingently sensibilized.

Virtue cannot be derived from a possessory state. Designe contains its own good and evil. In a possessory Being-in-the-World the actor can see only the opportunistic orders of appearance. He pits the chanciness of optative calculation against these representations. The judgments of prudence modify the chanciness of practical choice. In this manner does matter seek to impose itself on matter in a possessory order. In this manner, too, does virtue become irrelevant to both designe and action. Neither good nor evil can be placed in such an order of Being-in-the-World. The Hobbesian prudent knows preferentially, but not normatively. The formative potency of the imagination has been made subservient to preference.

The non-possessory order is not an optative Being-in-the-World. It is not an order of acting or of being acted upon. It is not an order to which prudence has any relevance. As an order of intelligibility about matter, it is an interrogative order. Its potency is the order in the world that can be generated by its interrogativeness. If, for the Hobbesian prudent, the world of matter can be known by its attributes of sense, then, for the Aristotelian prudent, the world of matter can also be known by its intelligible aspects, and that is enough for a more universal and truer knowing of the substance of the things of matter. The non-possessory, interrogative knowing of the Aristotelian prudent, with its employment of the imagic for a knowing that is not representational, is a formative potency that is not subservient to designe.

REFERENCES

1. *Hobbes's Leviathan*—(Rep. of Ed. of 1651, Oxford University Press 1909, Imp. of 1929)

2. *Aristotle's Metaphysics*—(Hippocrates G. Apostle, Transl.and Comm., Indiana University Press, 1966)

3. *Aristotle, De Anima*—(R. D. Hicks, Transl. and Notes, Cambridge University Press, 1907)

CHAPTER X

Being and Prudential Knowing

THE POSSESSORY ORDER of the Hobbesian prudent has its own gnostics. The avoidance of overknowing is a way of staking out its own gnostic boundaries. Sensibilized representations are not to be taken back beyond antecedent and consequence, as contingent appearances, to a causal order of things in the world. As it is, enough is disclosed to sensibilization for designe to set a "trayne" of thoughts in motion. Beyond this point there is no necessity for knowing more about an order of things in the world, even though there is the beckoning curiosity of self-interest.

Being and Subjectness

What is necessary is a corrective knowing by which the actor can come to judgment about his own designe and his own appetancy. The acquired reasoning capability that is a calculative reasoning supplies the analytic for corrective knowing. Analytic knowing does not determine Being-in-the-World, but is subordinate to it. It is imagination that invests Being-in-the-World with the constitutive elements from which designe will form the constitutive order for Being-in-the-World. Fancy (imagination) and judgment (reason), as constrained by prudence (experience), become transformed into the preference and predictions of what is chosen as both conducive to felicity and possible as outcomes.

Desire as a drive state reigns in that interval of time between the imagined pre-materialization underlying designe and the actuality of a future good materialized as a possessory present.

Neither at this point, nor at any point prior or subsequent, is Being of any relevance and, hence, of any concern to the prudence of a possessory order. Being—just Being—Being alone, Being by itself, without more. The Hobbesian prudent is an actor without Being. He is there in his materiality of form and his attributes of sense, the edifice of existence on which all else is constructed, and from which all else is derived. He is there in his magnitude and his activity and his passions and his sensibilized thought. The Hobbesian prudent is an actor of whom it can be predicated that there are qualities and attributes of his existence as matter, and by resort to which both his gnostics and his potencies as an agent of action are to be explicated. But he is without Being.

Without Being, there is no underlying subject. In its unqualified or "primary sense," Aristotelian Being "signifies whatness and a *this*." Without this "whatness" there is no substance. All predication of qualities and attributes imply "the underlying subject; and this is the substance and the individual, which is indicated in the corresponding predication." (1:108, Bk Z) In and of itself, matter is not the "whatness" or essence of the underlying subject. "The essence of each thing is what the thing is said to be in virtue of itself . . . and essence will belong primarily and in the full sense to a substance." (1:111-12 Bk Z)

In the case of the Hobbesian prudent, his gnostics and his potencies are explicated without resort to Being. The predicates of that which has the substantiality of matter is sufficient for explication. In such explication, "matter" refers to "that which in itself is not stated as being the whatness of something nor a quantity, nor any of the other senses of being." (1:100 Bk Z) In the case of the Aristotelian prudent, Being enters into the explication of his gnostics and his potencies. With Being, in other words, the three questions must be dealt with: 1) How does matter make itself known to other matter? 2) How does matter impose itself on other matter? 3) Why does matter impose itself on other matter?

Being and Knowing

Hobbesian gnostics, as has been seen, emerges as a determinate knowing about these three questions. The Aristotelian gnostics of Being, as will be seen, emerges as an indeterminate knowing about these three questions. There is, at the outset, the notion of soul. "Now the soul is that whereby primarily we live, perceive, and have understanding." (2:57 Ch 2) Of the notion of soul, Kant has written:

> Neither experience nor rational inference gives us adequate grounds for deciding whether man has a soul (in the sense of a substance dwelling in him, distinct from the body and capable of thinking independently of it, i.e., a spiritual substance), or whether it is not much rather the case that life may be a property of matter. (3:418)

The point of it all is that life as a property of matter—the Aristotelian notion of soul—leaves something of prudence to be extracted from within that interpenetrating unit of physico-biologic matter. The philosophic appraisal of Niels Bohr, drawn from atomic physics, is not destructive of the Aristotelian use of the notion of soul to deal analytically with life as a property of matter. Bohr took note that, on the one hand, there is acceptance of the "belief that no proper understanding of the essential aspects of life is possible in purely physical terms." He also took note that, on the other hand, there is the rejection of vitalism, a view whose assumption is "that a peculiar vital force, unknown to physics, governs all organic life." (4:9) Suppose, however, the viewpoint advocated is that research could remedy the absence of those "fundamental traits (which) are still missing in the analysis of natural phenomena" and whose absence bars reaching "an understanding of life on the basis of physical experience." (4:8) It is not a defensible viewpoint, Bohr concluded, because:

> In every experiment on living organisms there must remain some uncertainty as regards the physical conditions to which they are subjected, and the idea suggests itself that the minimal freedom we must allow the organism will be just large enough to permit it, so to say, to hide its ultimate secrets from us. On this view, the very existence of life must in biology be considered as an elementary fact, just as in atomic physics the existence of the quantum of action has to be taken as a basic fact that cannot be derived from ordinary mechanical physics. (4:9)

Being introduces into Thinking a knowing that is neither representational nor conceptual, neither sensibilized nor speculative. Just as designe, for the Hobbesian prudent, initiates, calls for, and gives directionality to thinking, so too, does Being, for the Aristotelian prudent, initiate, call for, and give directionality to Thinking. Being is not the intellect. It is not reason autonomous. But it is because of Being that there is an underlying subject with a particular kind of knowing. Sensibilized representations are a particular kind of knowing, the "simple apprehension by Thought." (2:141 Ch. 7) The concepts of speculative intellect are a particular kind of knowing, the intelligible aspects of matter. What is the particular kind of knowing that the underlying subject introduces into thinking because of the quiddity or whatness of Being?

Being As A Pre-emptive Potency

Being is the source of a pre-emptive potency of reason or intellect. Hobbesian designe regulates the succession and focus of thought, but it is a regulation that is unbounded because designe itself is without boundaries. The regulativeness that has its source in designe is subservient to the possessory. The possessory, in turn, is subservient to the correctiveness of calculative reasoning. Both designe and calculative reasoning are concerned with the predicates of materiality; take, that is, the sensibilized matter as a substance (reality) of actuality. This is the knowing from which are derived the conditions for the understanding of experience. That understanding emerges as a contingently logical naturalism. All matter exists in its appearance as natural phenomena. All relationships are connections with matter or between matter, and hence are also natural phenomena. No normative boundaries on designe exist with respect to natural phenomena. The only limits are those of preference and capability.

What Being brings into the play of thinking (reason) is the knowledge that the formative potency of imagination and designe can bring into creation that which had not previously existed as actuality. This capability whereby formative potency can bring into existence an actuality is the capability to create an order of things. Being is the source of a pre-emptive potency with respect to the creation of an order of things as an actuality of existence. This pre-emptive potency is the pre-emptive potency of the normative as reason. The source of this pre-emptive potency is Being in its primary sense of quiddity or whatness. Hence it is that Being directs thinking to the order of things created or produced by action and to the agent of action.

> For in productive sciences the principle of a thing produced is in that which produces, whether this is intellect or art or some power, and in practical sciences the principle of *action* is in the doer, and this is *choice*; for that which is done and that which is *chosen* are the same thing. (1:102 Bk E)

So it is that Aristotle wrote with respect to prudence not only that it needs knowledge both of general truths and of particular facts" (5:192 Bk VI), but also "that it is impossible to be prudent without being morally good." (5:205 Bk VI)

Being and Prudence

By making Being an integral part of prudence, Aristotelian prudence does three things. First, it fuses virtue—"Moral virtue"—

into prudence. Hobbesian prudence, with its contingently logical naturalism, had made a virtue-less experience the essence of prudence. Second, it tied virtue—moral virtue—to gnostics. The "morally good" involves a particular kind of knowing. Third, it answers the question: Why does matter impose itself on other matter? Because of virtue. The response of the Hobbesian prudent to this question is: Because of the passions. Aristotelian prudence introduces, through Being, a pre-emptive potency respecting the creation of an order of things.

What is the gnostics of Being? Given Being, that is, how does matter make itself known to other matter? The answer of the Hobbesian prudent is through the materialization of its appearance in the present as a evanescent interval of time between the past and the future. An order of things, however, must transcend time evanescent. It must exist in time transcendent; in a time that transcends the contingent materialization of the sensibilized present. Suppose, to deal with the gnostics of time transcendent, the term "presence"—the term used by Heidegger—is substituted for sensibilization so that something more than simple representation is known because of Being.

Volitional Time and Fateful Thinking

Being knows time volitionally, not passively.

> Since long ago, that which is present has been regarded as what is. But what representational ideas can we form of what in a way is no longer, and yet still is? What ideas can we form of that which was? At this 'it was,' idea and its willing take offence. Faced with what 'was' willing no longer has anything to say. Faced with every 'it was,' willing no longer has anything to propose. This 'it was' resists the willing of that will. The 'it was' becomes a stumbling block for all willing. (6:92)

Being knows time volitionally. The past and the future, therefore, have volitional presence in the will of present existence. Memory as "thinking that recalls"—rather than a passive capacity for retention—is a preservation of what provokes thought, and thus "what must be thought about." (6:151) What must be thought about is fateful thinking. Fateful thinking is thinking that "sees." The thinking of Hobbesian prudence is fateless thinking. It thinks only of the possessory outcomes of its own designes. It does not "see" otherwise than the calculation by which to make these consequences determinate. Aristotelian prudence recognizes a nonseeing cleverness that is latent in calculation.

The thinking that has its origins in the initiative, the calling, and the directionality of Being also "sees." It sees, through "presence" that which emerges from its concealment into the "lying-before-us" of being present. This presencing is not the attribute objectivity and reality of matter. Rather, as Heidegger put it:

> Wherever the thinking of the Greeks gives heed to the presence of what is present, the traits of presence which we mentioned find expression: unconcealedness, the rising from unconcealedness, the entry into unconcealedness, the coming and the going away, the duration, the gathering, the radiance, the rest, the hidden suddenness of possible absenting. These are the traits of presence in whose terms the Greeks thought of what is present. (6:237)

Fateful thinking is directed to seeing and judging the ambiguous "concealedness" and "the coming into present being and being present" of orders of things.

Hobbesian "Seeing" and Calculative Thinking

In the determined effort to avoid overknowing, the Hobbesian prudent becomes committed to engaging in under-knowing. It is an under-knowing that is the outcome of what the Hobbesian prudent permits himself to "see," and also the outcome of not recognizing that prudential thought and prudential action are those of an underlying subject. The restriction of "seeing" to the knowing of present appearance only (only the present has a being in nature) is underknowing. Only an isolated event/phenomenon is disclosed as appearance and known as a present representation.

The present is either on or it is off, in terms of its being in nature. The what is to be next—the future—is only a fiction of the mind, a presumption. The Hobbesian prudent does not "see" how an order of things reveals itself. Nor does he "see" how an order of things is willed by an underlying subject to be revealed. He does not trust the future. It is the cause of anxiety about his own fortunes. He is driven by his under-knowing "to assure for ever, the way of his future desire." (7:76) Calculative thinking and a ceaseless quest for one power after another are conjoined.

What intrudes into the prudence of the Hobbesian actor is the obligation that the prudential pierce the veil which obscures its "seeing."

> Aim, view, field of vision, mean here both the sight beheld and seeing, in a sense that is determined from out of Greek thought, but that has undergone the change of *idea* from *eidos* to *perceptio*. Seeing is that representing which since Leibniz has been grasped more explicitly in terms of its fundamental characteristic of striving (*appetitus*). All being whatever is a putting forward or setting forth . . . (8:72)

The "signes" antecedent and consequent of the "seeing" of the Hobbesian prudent are what is seen, but they are signs that are seen without a point of view. Not until the entry of "designe" is there a point of view for "seeing." The prior signs antecedent and consequent are not signs of the calculable. For the Hobbesian prudent, these prior signs are absent the objectivity that can be fitted into calculative thinking.

> All calculation makes the calculable 'come out' in the sum so as to use the sum for the next count. Nothing counts for calculation save what can be calculated. Any particular thing is only what it 'adds up to,' and any count ensures the further progress of the counting . . . The 'coming out' of the calculation with the help of what-is counts as the explanation of the latter's Being. Calculation uses everything that 'is' as units of computation, in advance, and, in the computation uses up its stock of units. The consumption of what-is reveals the consuming nature of calculation . . . it is of the prime-essence of calculation, and not merely in its results, to assert what is only in the

form of something that can be arranged and used up. Calculative thought places itself under compulsion to master everything in the logical terms of its procedure. (9:387-88)

Prudential "seeing" has to deal with the world as it appears in the form of the signs of the non-calculable as well as with its appearance in the form of the signs of the calculable. The Hobbesian prudent has put to one side the signs antecedent and consequent that are prior to designe. Until then there is no "Trayne of regulated thoughts." (7:20) Until then, there is only that "Mentall Discourse" which is "*Unguided, without* Designe." (7:19) The difference between thought before designe and thought after designe is in terms of the presence or absence of "Passionate Thought, to govern and direct those that follow, to itself, as the end and scope of some desire, or other passion." (7:19)

Passionate and Meditative Thought

The "passionate thought" of the Hobbesian prudent can be set against the "meditative thought" of the Aristotelian prudent. Each represents a type of gnostics of materiality, a mode whereby materiality knows materiality. Even as to that unguided and less "constant" thinking—the thinking without designe—the Hobbesian prudent concedes that "yet in this wild ranging of the mind, a man may oft-times perceive the way of it, and the dependance of one thought upon another." (8:19) The regulativeness of designe constrains "passionate thought" to the calculable what-is of present representation. "Passionate thought," to use the words of Heidegger, "Binds itself to the calculation of what-is and ministers to this alone." (9:387)

Yet the world also reveals itself to the prudent in "The slow signs of the incalculable." (9:391) There is thus a revealing of more than the what-is, on which alone does designe focus "passionate thought," because of that which is to be brought about as an effect through activity by an efficient cause. Prudence is concerned with the whole of revealing or "unconcealment" with respect to the world of Being, and not with just the object representation of sensibilized appearance. This revealing is the coming to presence.

> Wherever man opens his eyes and ears, unlocks his heart, and gives himself over to meditating and striving, shaping and working, entreating and thanking, he finds himself everywhere already brought into the concealed. This unconcealment of the unconcealed has already come to pass whenever it calls man forth into the modes of revealing alloted to him. (8:18-19)

The meditative is a thinking that hovers, as against a thinking that only represents. The meditative is a thinking in which the world is more than a picture of imagined representations. The meditative is a thinking in which thought is released from subordination to perception. The meditative is a thinking in which all relation is not a relation to what is represented. The meditative is a thinking in which the real is not just the outcome that is the result following from the operational acts of an efficient cause done in a particular sequence in time. The meditative is a kind of thinking in which the real is not solely the factual certainty of consequences. (8: Pt. III)

The meditative is a thinking that hovers. It hovers about that which does not make an appearance in the subject-object relationships of representation. It hovers about that which does not appear in the perception of signs antecedent and consequent. It hovers about that which enters into the time frame of Being as more than, and as other than, the knowing of a sensibilized objectified present. The meditative is a thinking that hovers reflectively. The meditative is a reflective "seeing."

Virtue, Passionless Thought and Prudential Knowing

"It is evident," wrote Aristotle toward the end of his exposition of *The Intellectual Virtues*, "that it is impossible to be good in the full sense without prudence, or to be prudent without moral virtue." He continues on

> . . . The presence of the single virtue of prudence implies the presence of all the moral virtues.
>
> And thus it is plain, in the first place, that, even if it did not help practice, we should yet need prudence as the virtue or excellence of a part of our nature; . . . (5:206-7 Bk VI)

Aristotelian prudence ties virtue to knowing, to prudential knowing or the knowing of prudence. No logical naturalism of the Hobbesian prudent, by way of contrast, can tie virtue to knowing. Moral virtue, for the Hobbesian prudent, has nothing to do with gnostics. The good of moral virtue is unnecessary for any analytic ordering of signs antecedent and consequent in relation to what has been imagined by designe. Hobbesian virtue is the equivalent of passionless thought, and appetitive indifference towards the world. With passionless thought there is no designe over and against the world.

Passionless thought is thereby unable to impose a logical ordering of relations between phenomena as representations. An ordering of this kind—the product of an analytic mode of calculative reasoning—is indispensable for the possessory stance that is epitomized by designe. "Passionate thought" is the necessary condition for the objectification of the world. "Passionate thought" is the necessary condition for reducing the world to the particular certainty that is demanded by the specific opportunity contained within the imagination of designe. The facticity of objectification and the analytical coherence of objectified phenomena establish a logical comprehension of the relations between representations. This logical comprehension is the order of things for logical materialism. As even Hobbes himself conceded (7:Ch. V), the objectification of the world by "passionate thought" leads to science. Thus it leads to a theory of reality in the world described by Heidegger in the following terms:

> Science sets upon the real. It orders it into place to the end that at any given time the real will exhibit itself as an interacting network, i.e., in surveyable series of related causes. The real thus becomes survey-

able and capable of being followed out in its sequences. The real becomes secured in its objectness. From this there result spheres or areas of objects that scientific observation can entrap after its fashion. Entrapping representation, which secures everything in that objectness which is thus capable of being followed out, is the fundamental characteristic of the representing through which modern science corresponds to the real. (8:168 Pt. III)

The Good

The good that is not the "apparent good" of the consequence of acting upon designe, the good of "moral virtue," is included within Aristotelian prudence. It is the good that is introduced into prudence by Being. It is unlike the expectation of a consequent good that is introduced into Hobbesian prudence as an acolyte of designe. Hobbesian designe is the employment of the imagination in the service of willing an outcome (an episode of materialization) into existence or actuality. The good of Aristotelian prudence satisfies a condition whereby Being can comprehend an order of things in which experience is enframed. Aristotelian prudence knows an order of things that are of significance with respect to Being. It knows more than the logical naturalism of an order of subject-object relations. It knows something different than the hosted expectations that are the calculated outcomes of Hobbesian prudence. The trap for the good of "moral virtue" is to make it a derivative of one more competitive, analytically calculative method, or to make it a discrete factor in calculative reasoning.

Calculative Materialization

All calculation extracts from, by passing through, a pool of objectified information. It is by this mode that calculation uses up that which it has objectified on behalf of designe. All calculating takes that which is to be created—produced as an episode of materialization by an acting subject as efficient cause—as a consequent of the what-is of logical naturalism. All calculation culminates in a determinate outcome—matter imposing itself on matter, by acting and being acted upon. All episodes of materialization—all creations of an order in the world by acting subjects— are not simply consequents, but are also an unconcealing about the world of existence. The meditative is a hovering about this unconcealing through episodes of materialization. The "moral virtue" of Aristotelian prudence is a revealing. However, as against the determinate outcome that is ever the ultimate culmination of Hobbesian designe, "moral virtue" is indeterminacy writ large, and nothing more than another preference.

The Good of Moral Virtue

The good of "moral virtue" is tied to an order of things and not to an object of thought regulated by designe. The good of "moral virtue" is part of Being-in-the-World and not an idea about the world. The meditative as a hovering that reveals is a knowledge about an order of things in the world that is revealing itself as a presence to Being. The order of things in the world is both an object of knowledge and knowledge of the object.

> . . . is it not in some cases *knowledge* and its object are the same? In the productive sciences, this object is the *substance* or the essence but without the matter, in the theoretical sciences it is the formula and the thought. Accordingly, since the intellect and the object of thought are not distinct in things which have no matter, the two will be the same, and so both thought and the object of thought will be one. (1:210 Bk A)

The good that is the "moral virtue" of Aristotelian prudence is a knowing that is neither optatively calculative simply because of its sensibilization, nor pure gnostics as idea only. It is not the latter, because ideas as pure gnostics would make the good of "moral virtue" separate from and anterior to persons as sensible substances. The untenableness of this position has been demonstrated by Aristotle.

> They (those who "posit the ideas as being universal substances and at the same time as separate and as individuals") thought that the individuals among sensible things are in a state of flux and that none of them is permanent, but that the universal exists apart from these and is something distinct from them. As we said earlier, Socrates began thinking in this direction because of his inquiry into definitions; however, he did not separate these from the individuals, and he thought rightly in not doing so. This is brought out by the facts; for without the universal it is not possible to acquire *knowledge*, but the separation of the universal from the individuals is the cause of the difficulties that arise with regard to the Ideas. The exponents of the Ideas, however, thinking, that, if indeed there are to be any substances besides the sensible and ever-changing ones, they must exist separately, had no others to put forward but the so-called 'universal substances'; and so the universal substances turn out to be of about the same nature as the individual substances. (1:234, Bk M)

The good of "moral virtue" is the gnostics of an order because it is a knowing of relationality. "All things are ordered someway," wrote Aristotle. Differences between orders exist, but as to these orders, "they do not exist without being related at all to one another, but they are in some way related. For all things are ordered in relation to one thing." (1:210, Bk A) Relationality directs knowing to the nature of the whole order. It is in "the nature of the whole" that "good and the highest good" exists. Actors generate and maintain an order. An order exists because of the actors, and actors exist within an order of things. Aristotle accepted the position of those Greek thinkers who "regard the *Good* as a principle, but they do not say how it is a principle, whether as an end or as a mover or as form." (1:211, Bk A)

An order and its relationality is a more ultimate perception than an object of sensibility. Aristotelian prudence makes "seeing" more than a sensibilized representation. The "seeing" of Aristotelian prudence is an apprehending or mode of knowing. Aristotle noted that the calculative could be separated out from "seeing," so that the former could be done independently of the latter. A non-prudential calculative is therefore possible. Aristotelian prudence also "sees" not only "the good," but the more ultimate or "highest good." It is in the relationality that is an order of things that the more ultimate good exists. Not only the what-is of present objectification, but the order of things that exists also has a being in nature. Being-in-the-World is existence within an order of things, the presence of which is a revealing, disclosing, unconcealing. The "seeing" of Aristotelian prudence is the perception of the more ultimate good as a pre-emptive regulator of prudential thinking. Here is the "right reason" that infuses into purpose "a certain moral character or state of the desires" (5:183, Bk VI) and that makes prudence "adopt the right means to the end." (5:207, Bk VI)

REFERENCES

1. Aristotle's *Metaphysics*—(Hippocrates G. Apostle, Transl. and Comm., Indiana University Press 1966).

2. Aristotle—*DeAnima*—(R. D. Hicks, Transl. and Notes, Cambridge University Press 1907).

3. Kant, Immanuel—*The Doctrine of Virtue* (M. J. Gregor, Transl., Harper and Row, Torchbook 1964).

4. Bohr, Niels—*Atomic Physics and Human Knowledge* (John Wiley & Sons 1958).

5. *The Nicomachean Ethics of Aristotle*—(F. H. Peters Transl., Kegan Paul, Trench & Co., London 1884).

6. Heidegger, Martin—*What is Called Thinking* (Harper and Row 1968 ed.)

7. Hobbes's *Leviathan*—(Rep. of Ed. of 1651, Oxford University Press 1909, Imp. of 1929).

8. Heidegger, Martin—*The Question Concerning Technology* (W. Lovitt, Transl. and Intro., Harper Colophon, Harper & Row 1977).

9. Heidegger, Martin—*Existence and Being* (H. Regnery Co., Chicago 1949).

CHAPTER XI

The Worldhood of Prudence

I.
WORLDHOOD WITHOUT NATURE

Action, for the Hobbesian prudent, does not require any reflection about nature. At the same time, the Hobbesian prudent must extricate his actions from that which is going on in nature. The efficient cause of the Hobbesian prudent does not permit of any explanation of nature in terms of the "naturall causes of things." (1:81) And this despite an acknowledged inquisitiveness on the part of the Hobbesian prudent as to the causes of events. He remains in ignorance both of "remote causes" and of "naturall causes." Curiosity about the latter passes into a futile progression from the cause of the cause of particular effects to an empty Diety of eternal cause.

For the Hobbesian prudent to extricate his actions from that which is going on in nature, he must extricate the explanation of action from the grip of space-time binding of events. The certainty that buttresses the efficient cause of the Hobbesian prudent lies in the experience of events in a temporal order. It is only an experiential certainty. It lies in the "observation and memory of the order, consequence and dependence of the things they see: Man observeth how one Event hath been produced by another; and remembreth in them Antecedence and Consequence." (1:82)

He is inclined to introduce an efficient cause into this temporal order of events, "a cause which determined the same to begin, when it did, rather than sooner or later"; in short, an explanatory cause. Nevertheless, as to antecedent and consequence, the Hobbesian prudent has only an experiential certainty, and not a cognitive or epistemological certainty.

The observed signs that establish the experiential certainty of temporal relationships between antecedent and consequent events by which the actor may "guesse at the Future time" is only the prudence of Thinking Animals.(2) For the Hobbesian prudent, "it is not the prudence that distingueth man from beast." (1:22) The Hobbesian prudent is not curious about the truth of "naturall causes." What he takes to be the universal object of curiosity by prudent actors are the "causes of good and evill fortune." (1:82) Here "The Trayn of regulated thoughts" is such that "when imagining anything whatsoever, we seek all the possible effects, that can be produced; that is to say, we imagine what we can do with it, when we have it." (1:20) It is this which leads to the prudence that is peculiar to man. It is the prudence of the actor who observes both how things conduce to a "designe", and to what "designe" they may be conduced by his actions. (1:55) It is, moreover, the prudence that extricates the actor from the primal animality of thinking about the future only in terms of the space-time binding of events.

Blind Nature and Purpose-Serving Events

The nature that is a futile object of thought for the Hobbesian prudent has nevertheless been transformed by him into the worldhood of prudential action. The nature of the Hobbesian prudent is a blind nature, but one which in the blindness of its motion brings forth the events that can serve as the raw material for prudential action. Nature cooperates, so to speak, in a physical explanation of action. Moving out from his own explanatory ground, the Hobbesian prudent intersects with an aspect of nature also relevant for the Aristotelian prudent, moving out from his own explanatory ground. What the Aristotelian prudent recognizes is the existence of purpose-serving events, the matter having been stated by Aristotle as follows:

> . . . of events some serve a purpose (whether they take place as the result of purpose or not), while others do not; so that among unusual events some may serve a purpose. Events that serve a purpose are those that might proceed from thought or from nature. When such events take place *per accidens,* we ascribe them to chance. (3:353-354)

Memory and Recollection

Memory and remembrance are used interchangeably by the Hobbesian prudent to explain the cognizing of purpose-serving events. For the Aristotelian prudent, however, memory is to be distinguished from recollection. The latter has a different conception of the relation of perception to thought than the former. It is this difference that leads to distinguishing memory from recollection.

For both prudents, the sensory perceptions of the past provide the subject matter for memory. Still, the Hobbesian conception of memory as "decaying sense," or the images of sense that are "fading, old, and past" (1:14) is not identical with the Aristotelian conception of memory. The Aristotelian conception makes memory not of sense, but a "faculty of sense"; that is, the faculty by which the actor perceives "the lapse of time." (4:237) Memory, or remembrance, relates to a sensory image in time. All sensation must be of that which has extension in space and exists in time. There is a primal sensory animality to remembering in time, because "extent and movement must be apprehended by the same faculty as time is, so that knowledge of extent, movement and time must be due to the primary faculty of sense." (4:235) True enough, there is a lapse of time between sensation and memory. This time-lapse, however, introduces a modification of the sensory experience. "Thus memory is neither sensation nor judgment, but a modification of these due to a time-lapse." (4:235)

In remembering there is the duality of remembering that which is presently being experienced, or the remembering of the past experience in which the present experience has its origins. No past sensation can exist in the present, but it can exist as an object of thought. The subject matter of memory can be "taken both to be something in itself and to be something else. In itself it is an object of contemplation or an image, but inasmuch as it is of something else it is a likeness and a reminder." (4:236)

Recollection has a different significance for action than has memory. While memory is linked to sensory perception (5:71), where it is also left by the Hobbesian prudent, recollection is linked by the Aristotelian prudent to experiential knowing. The link between recollection and knowing extends the action of the Aristotelian prudent beyond the confines of the space-time binding of primal sensory animality. "While many other animals remember, virtually no known animal but man recollects." (4:242) (8:71)

For the Aristotelian prudent, experiencing involves a state of knowing. In consequence, experience is treated as the equivalent of knowledge. The contrast with the Hobbesian prudent is that for the latter "Much memory . . . is called Experience" (1:14), so that experience is identified with memory of previous perceptions. For the Aristotelian prudent, by the way of contrast, much experience is called knowledge. Recollection is the action useful recovery of previous knowledge, without having either to relearn it or having to undergo a recurrence of the original experience. More than the remembered sensibility of perceptions of time-lapse and the movement of objects in space is involved in recollection. That "more" is a reasoned principle of knowing.

> The reason is that recollecting is a sort of reasoning; that we have previously seen, heard, etc. is known by reasoning, and a sort of search is involved. This naturally occurs only in beings which can deliberate for deliberation is also a sort of reasoning. (4:242)

Hobbesian Causality

The Hobbesian prudent is searching out purpose-serving events. He is searching them out in the chance occurrence of nature. The causality of concern to the Hobbesian prudent has nothing to do with nature. Hobbesian causality is that of the agent searching for the causes of his own good and evil fortune. He searches by the observed signs of prudence; "But the signes of prudence are all uncertain, because to observe by experience, and remember all circumstances that may alter the successe, is impossible." (1:38) The position of the Hobbesian actor is one of which the Aristotelian prudent is cognizant:

> . . . For chance events can happen only to beings capable of having good fortune, and, in general, of acting; as is indicated by the fact that good fortune is thought to be almost if not quite the same as 'doing well', which is a kind of action.
>
> Hence no lifeless thing or lower animal or child can *act* by chance, because it has not purpose; nor can such beings have good or bad fortune except in a merely analogous sense. . . .
>
> . . . chance is found when a purpose serving result happens spontaneously to a being that has purpose. (3:354-55)

The action of the Hobbesian actor is action in accordance with a naturalistic philosophy of prudence. It is thus because the action of the Hobbesian actor is grounded in the materiality of the physical explanation of action. Yet he is without knowledge of the principles of the materiality of the nature that supplies him with purpose-serving events. The Hobbesian actor has a naturalistic explanation of action, but not a philosophy of nature. It is because of the latter that the Hobbesian actor has an explanation of action which, while materialistic, has no fundament in an explanation of nature. Hobbesian prudence thereby becomes the prudence of worldhood without nature.

II.
WORLDHOOD WITH NATURE

Aristotelian prudence, in contrast, is the prudence of a worldhood with nature. The materiality for the physical in the explanation of action is supplied by nature. The action of the Aristotelian prudent, however, is action taken with knowledge of the principles of the materiality of the nature that supplies him with purpose-serving events. He has a philosophy of nature that supplies him with an explanation of what is the materiality that enters into an explanation of action.

Nature As Telic Causality

Nature is not just motion, as it is for the Hobbesian prudent, but those things or substances in which nature exists as "a principle of motion and rest." (3:349) The things of nature exist not only as matter, but as "things that have an internal principle of change." (Ibid.) The exclusivity of the interest of the Hobbesian prudent in the efficient cause of change focuses attention on only "the sequence of events, and in determining the proximate agent." (3:356) In the explanatory terms of the Hobbesian prudent:

> Ignorance of remote causes, disposeth men to attribute all events, to the causes immediate, and instrumentall: For these are all the causes they perceive. (1:80)

Nor is the nature of the Aristotelian prudent considered to be a blind nature, a nature without purpose and end. "Nature . . . is a cause, and one that works towards an end." (3:358) The things of nature, the things in which nature exists as an internal principle of change, exhibit an "adaptation to ends" that appears as activity "which looks like the work of reason." (3:357) No temporal explanation of the physicality of these activities in terms of antecedent and consequent can explain them as events which follow necessarily from what has preceded. Even the indentification of purpose with motive and deliberation—the hallmarks of the human causal agent—does not rule out nature as exhibiting a kind of intelligence. Motive is supplied by the presence of "the motive principle," or the principle of change, in the things of nature themselves. Nature does not require deliberation in order for it to be purposive. The things of nature exhibit "a course of action" which terminates in "end-like results." For the Aristotelian prudent:

> Where there is a terminus to a course of action, the earlier stages are for the sake of the terminus. Now the course of nature corresponds to the course of action. Therefore the course of nature also is for an end. (3:357)

The Hobbesian prudent starts and completes action within the conception of actuality. The Aristotelian prudent begins action within the conception of actuality, but completes it within the conception of potentiality. The Aristotelian "nature is just a principle of change." (3:359) Actuality and potentiality enter into the change that is produced by action. In its most generalized meaning, potentiality includes every principle of change. "Change may now be defined as the actualization of the potential as such." (3:359) Nature as the potentiality of "every principle of change or of rest" is then "a moving principle, not in another thing, but in the same thing qua itself." (6:154)

Actuality, Potentiality and Matter

The Hobbesian prudent, however, has made the motion of the matter that is materiality the explanation of change. Matter exists as motion for the Hobbesian prudent. Not so for the Aristotelian, for whom "matter does not exist in actuality, yet it does

The Worldhood of Prudence

exist potentially." (6:178) Motion cannot explain change, nor can it explain matter, "For every motion is incomplete." (6:152) Motion qua motion is incomplete because it leaves matter without form (that is, without an internal principle of change), and it leaves matter without substance, and it leaves action without end.

As to matter, "matter exists potentially in view of the fact that it might come to possess a form; and when it exists *actually*, then it exists in a form." (6:155) As to that which is being generated by action, "generation is for the sake of an end; and the end is an *actuality*, and potentiality is viewed as being for the sake of this." (6:155) The potency of action on the part of an agent becomes manifest in motion, but not the state of Being or existence of the agent of action, which is the essential of the actuality of substance.

Actuality is the starting ground for action by both Hobbesian and Aristotelian prudents. Actuality must precede potentiality in time, for capability or the potency of action, and the knowing or learning for action, must exist first in actuality. The difference between the two actors is that for the Hobbesian the ground for action is actuality without potentiality, while for the Aristotelian it is actuality with potentiality.

The future cannot exist as potentiality for the Hobbesian prudent, because the future cannot be envisaged as the actuality of matter in any sensible form. The Hobbesian future exists as "the way of his future desire." (1:75) Nor is the action of the Hobbesian prudent encompassed within the conception of final ends. There is no "*Finis Ultimus*" and no "*Summum Bonum*" for the Hobbesian actor. And it is his position, too, that no person can "any more live, whose Desires are at an end, than he, whose Senses and Imagination are at a stand." (1:75)

Actuality, Potentiality and Action

All Hobbesian ends are instrumental. There is no potentiality in instrumental ends. Their actuality lies in their potency for the attainment of what it is that is desired. "Felicity" is the time related measure of the progression of the Hobbesian prudent from one desired actuality to another desired actuality. The prior actuality is but instrumental, "being still but the way to the latter." (1:75) Felicity measures the potency of the actuality of any instrumental end for attaining future desires, which is the actuality of performance outcomes. In the case of instrumental ends, the end is always the performance of certain actions. Hobbesian performance—which is its own end—is the prior actuality by which still another later actuality is generated for action in the way of future desire. All such desire is the desire of the Hobbesian for the actuality of that desired.

The Hobbesian prudent derives pleasure from the sense or appearance of Good, which Good is no more than the reckoned consequences of action in relation to the desires and aversions of the actor. It is an apparent Good because the actor is unable to see through to the end of the chain of consequences of actions. The actuality of desire is a possessory Good. Present means as a power to bring into actuality that future possessory Good is the potency of efficient cause. (1:42, 48).

Chance and Purpose-Serving Events

The Hobbesian prudent acts with reference to purpose-serving "end-attaining events." He sees either the designe to which events lead, or the designe to which they can be put. The events of nature conjoin with thought, or the events of thought conjoin with those of nature. Hence the Aristotelian statement "Events that serve a purpose are those that might proceed from thought or from nature." (3:353-54) The chance element of purpose-serving events is their incalculability. It is this incalculability that leads the Hobbesian prudent to ascribe an accidental causation to chance events. But, for the Aristotelian prudent:

Chance, then, is an accidental cause in the purposive subdivision of

> end-attaining events. Hence it is concerned with the same class of events as thought is . . .
>
> Chance is called good when some thing good results, evil when something evil. When a great good results or a great evil is just missed, that is good fortune; evil fortune is the reverse of this.
>
> Chance, and therefore good fortune, is rightly called insecure; for no chance event can be invariable or usual. (3:354)

The good fortune that is the "Felicity" of the Hobbesian prudent is insecure. Good fortune, or the way of future desire, cannot be made secure once and for all, or all at once. The assurance of future desire is the object of thought, and thought is itself regulated by desire. The Hobbesian "Trayne of regulated thoughts" conceptualizes nature in thought as the source of the accidental causation to be found in purpose-serving events. These events can be sequenced within a temporal order as antecedent and consequent. The action of the agent as efficient cause is the activity of performance by which there is generated the change that actualizes the object of desire. Nature is without explanation. Nature is not thought of as a kind of intelligence working for an end. While the Aristotelian classifies purpose as only a subdivision of end-attaining events, the Hobbesian has made purpose the entire equivalent of end. In consequence, nature is not thought of by the Hobbesian prudent as exhibiting end-attaining events. The actuality of matter as present materiality excludes matter as potentiality. The concentration is on matter; there is no place for substance.

The Aristotelian prudent, in contrast to the Hobbesian prudent, relates actuality to potentiality. It is not only that for the former change is "defined as the actualization of the potential as such." (3:350) Beyond this

> . . . it is evident that potential things are discovered by being brought to *actuality*. The cause of this is the fact that thinking is an *actuality*. And so it is by *actuality* that the potential becomes actual; and because of this we come to know by acting. . . . (6:158)

III.
THE DUALITY OF FUTURES

Actuality, Potentiality and Change

While change actualizes, actuality is prior to change. Potentiality is capable of becoming actual, but it may not exist in actuality. " . . . that which becomes actual by *thought* from existing potentially is this, that it becomes actual when *thought* wishes it and nothing external prevents this." (6:153) The regulation of potentiality is through actuality. Actuality is prior both to potentiality and to potency. This is the power of present means to obtain some future good. The potency of actuality selects, from that which potentially is capable of existing, that which will be in actuality. Potency is the principle of change in that which constitutes present means, as well as "the principle in virtue of which one accomplishes something well or according to *choice*." (6:87) Material things, in the potentiality of their capability, contain a contrariety of good and evil, being potentially capable of either. Hence, "a good *actuality* is better and more honorable than the potentiality for it," and "the actuality of what is bad is worse than the potentiality for it." (6:157)

Still, for the Hobbesian prudent, actuality is not a preemptive regulator of potentiality. The thought of the Hobbesian actor is not focused on potentiality, but on the kind of action by which to gain the desired good from the purpose-serving events that are by him perceived to exist as the actuality for action. Desire and deliberation have so conjoined as to confine his fore-seeing to the consequences of his own actions, not of potentiality.

Designe, Potentiality, and Futures

The Hobbesian prudent avowedly goes beyond that reasoning of animals which Hume long ago explicated as the expectations founded on past expericncc and that are the inferences of fact beyond present sensations. (7:IX) That is to say, what is introduced into thought by the Hobbesian prudent is "designe," which is derived from the imaginings of the actor about what can be done with anything to produce desired effects. (1:20) What limits the "designe" of the Hobbesian prudent is that potentiality cannot yet—as potential—be represented as a sense image. Potentiality does not have the facticality of the sensory present. Potentiality, therefore, presents an unconditioned aspect of future actuality.

Matter as actuality has a sense conditioned aspect. Its appearance to the Hobbesian actor as actuality is conditioned as a contingent fact of sense. It is the facticality of the sensory present. Matter as potentiality is not conditioned by the sensory present. Hence, as potentially, it has an unconditioned aspect, for it is absent the conditioned facticality of the sensorily present.

The future as change and as empirically possible events is not a future, but a *duality* of futures. One future consists of the effects of the Hobbesian prudent's analysis of purpose-serving events and the consequences of ensuing actions. The second future consists of the actualizing effects of the end-attaining events that exist as potentiality. Dual futures consists of two classes of futures. The class of alternate futures is one class. It is the outcome of selected variations in analysis by the Hobbesian prudent, analysis in which "the Appetites (Desire) and Aversions are raised by foresight of the good and evill consequences, and sequels of the action whereof we Deliberate." (3:48) The class of potentially foretended futures is the second class. Each of the two classes of dual futures contains a subdivision of end-attaining events. Potentiality has its own event time, whether the actuality of that which can be is realized through the agency of efficient cause, or realized through nature's own principles of realization.

REFERENCES

1. *Hobbes's Leviathan*—(Rep. of edition of 1651, Oxford University Press 1909, Imp. of 1929)

2. Shepard, Paul—*Thinking Animals: Animals and the Development of Human Intelligence* (Viking 1978)

3. Aristotle's *Physics*—(Ross, W.D. ed., Oxford University Press 1936)

4. Aristotle, *Parva Naturalia*, "De Memoria et Reminiscentia"—(Ross, W.D. ed., Oxford University Press 1955)

5. Sorabji, Richard—*Aristotle on Memory* (Brown University Press 1972) The author is critical of the connection by Aristotle of memory with perception such that memory is left with only an incidental connection to thought.

6. Aristotle's *Metaphysics*—(Hippocrates G. Apostle, Transl. and Comm., Indiana University Press 1966)

7. Hume, David—*An Inquiry Concerning Human Understanding* (1777 ed. Hendel, Chas. W. ed. Liberal Arts Press 1955)

CHAPTER XII

Prudence and the Worldhood of Temporality

I must resort to a contemporary and familiar (if rude) analogy and liken consciousness, or the neurophysiologic mechanism thereof, to a television tube with a so-called long decay time such that it continues to glow for a substantial period after it has been excited, and thus affords a continuous rather than a flickering image. Within the parameters of this image the conscious animal can relate past experiences to anticipated future and react accordingly; and with respect to one or another of various possibilities which may be presented simultaneously. Insofar as selectivity enters into this reaction we may speak of 'choice' without giving this much-abused word any metaphysical implications; and insofar as any of the alternative modes of action promote the organism's welfare, we may designate the resulting activity as 'self-serving.'

From the perspective of evolution, then, we may venture tentatively to define consciousness as awareness of environment and of self revealed objectively by self-serving neuro-muscular activity which exhibits choice between alternative actions and relates past experience to anticipated future. Whether the time-binding activity extends over a period of seconds or of years is immaterial to the cogency of the definition. (7:171)

Action and Time-Space Coding

Beneath the explanation of action by a human actor, whether it be action either by a Hobbesian or by an Aristotelian actor, lies what has been identified as "the biological anomaly of human thought." (1:15) What is biologically anomalous about it is the way in which human thought has ordered the world for action in terms of the time-space coding of its night time (or nocturnal) and daytime (or diurnal) mammalian ancestors. From the "Thinking Animals" who were nocturnal ancestors of human actors, there has evolved an ordering of the world for action in terms of sound and smell. From the "Thinking Animals" who were the diurnal ancestors of human actors, there has evolved an ordering of the world for action in terms of the stored products of vision.

Both sound and smell are a kind of information. Smell provides information about the close at hand. Sound, however, requires a succession of stimuli to arrive at a pattern of distance, movement, and direction of another. Perceiving these signals as a pattern, wrote Paul Shepard, meant ordering them in time rather than visual space, translating them into the all-at-once of a spatial map.

> . . . Though hearing and smell are not basically spatial, their temporal analysis creates a kind of analogue to space . . . The perception of patterns from signals coming at intervals meant holding what had gone before, putting it into a spatial code. (1:16)

Vision supplied a different relationship of time to space, although vision, too, would be based on a time-coding which was not dissimilar from that of sound. A perceptual visual world was created in which distance could mean time or space, and those events distant in time were remembered as mental images in the space of the mind's eye. The visual world became, as it were, constant or continuous rather "than an illuminated field, punctuated by the right signals." (1:17)

Hobbesian and Aristotelian actors are all thus in-the-world. It is a world that can be ordered in terms of a time-space coding. It is a world in which action is taken with reference to this coding. But it would not yet be action that could be explained in terms of the "worldhood" of the actors. (2:III) Thus far action would consist only of the acts of those who are in-the-world, but of whom it cannot yet be determined what it is that exists for them in the world. Explanation need not go as far as the primordiality of the "Being-in-the-World" of Heidegger. (2:I) Explanation, however, can go so far as to ascertain, in the case of Hobbesian and Aristotelian actors, what is action to their existence-in-the-world. In the case of both actors, there is a "Being-possible". (2:183)

The Actor As Entity Within-The-World

The spatiality that could be bound to time, the spatiality that Shepard found to be a "biological anomaly of human thought" in mammalian evolution (1:15), has its parallel in Cartesian thought. As traced by Heidegger, it was the influence of the philosophy of Descartes which separated that which is matter—the extended in space—from that which thinks. (2:122) The spatiality of material nature defined the constitutive actuality of the world—the reality that is fundamental for the actor-in-the-world. Motion, or movement, became a property of the materiality that is extended in space. Hence, as Heidegger put it, the motion of that which is matter must be experienced in terms of its being "conceived as a mere change of location." (2:124)

Additionally, the interpretation of the world of Cartesian materiality is always the interpretation of an actor who is of necessity "some entity within-the-world." (2:122) The space in which any actor is extended as a *res corporea* constitutes for that actor a limitation such that for him "the phenomenon of the world in general no longer comes into view." (2:122) The actor is within-the-world but without worldhood.

The Hobbesian prudent is an actor whose concept of prudence is contained within the negative concept of worldhood advanced by Descartes. The sensory capabilities of the Hobbesian actor—that which constituted his attributes as a material substance is "onely motion caused by the action of externall objects, but in apparence." (3:41) Moreover, the Hobbesian prudent has no concept of "the phenomenon of the world in general" as an order of things. Hobbesian prudents begin with where they are as entities within-the-world, and they work their way into prudential actions from an inquisitiveness "into the causes of the Events they see, some more, some lesse." (3:82)

Being prudents, Hobbesian actors are certain to go so far in their inquisitiveness as to "search of the causes of their own good and evill fortune." (3:82) The imposition of cause into the events they see introduces a certain sequentiality of time into perceived events. What had a beginning they "think also it had a cause, which determined the same to begin, then when it did, rather than sooner or later." (3:82) Time has now been bound to motion or events in space.

How does this time binding link into the actions of the Hobbesian prudent? The prudence of the Hobbesian actor "dependeth on much Experience, and Memory of the like Things, and their consequences heretofore." (3:55) But experience and memory are drawn upon only because the Hobbesian actor "has a designe in hand," and his thoughts "running over a multitude of things, observes how they conduce to that designe; or what designe they may conduce to." (3:55) As actor, the Hobbesian prudent has to consider both time in the sequence of perceived events, and time in the sequence of causality to be generated by his actions as a causal agent.

Cognized Time

Nevertheless, the Hobbesian actor has no theory of the events of nature in time. He is not interested in using time to describe natural events. He acts in time, but it is only a particular time in which he is interested. The time in which he is interested only comes into existence with consciousness of those events of which he becomes aware by virtue of "a designe in hand." The time of the Hobbesian actor is cognized time. It is time adapted to the phenomena existing in the "now" of consciousness and awareness. It is a relational time, one that exists, as Denbigh put it, "by reference to concrete events and thus to empirical states of the world (including states of consciousness)." (4:320)

The Hobbesian actor thinks about time as a derivative of the sensory conditions for cognizing about action. The material fundament of Hobbesian cognizing is sensation. Sensations are sequenced in time and they decay in time's decaying images of the Hobbesian actor. He has no notion of the passage of time. He has a temporal order in which decaying sense images represent the past. A sense based theory of action requires the decay of sense images to characterize a past as time past for present actions.

There is an Augustinian falling of the present into the past (5:341), because of a concept of the temporal order that has particular epistemological significance for action. As to such a temporal order, Denbigh has observed that it is a concept based "on the ability to distinguish between 'what-is-now' and 'what-is-in-the-Memory'—i.e., between 'now' and 'earlier than now.' More generally it is based on the ability to place known events in a series whose generating relation is 'earlier than.' " (4:319)

The future, lacking a sensory fundament, is less than real for the Hobbesian actor, because within such a temporal order there are no known events beyond the "now" of the actor. Known events are those with respect to which the actor has had a direct experience, and as to which, therefore, they can be placed by him in a relational series. The time that is the future for the Hobbesian actor is basically a "later than now." Given its temporal order, Hobbesian prudence becomes an anticipated serial relationship between the assumed events of later and now." Hobbesian prudence is indeed "a Praesumption of the *Future*, contracted from the *Experience* of time Past." (3:22) The future is a conjecture. In Denbigh's terms, "the temporal order as applied to any assumed events later than now ('future time') is a schematic construction." (4:319)

The cognized time of the Hobbesian actor, by which he places events in a serial relationship within a temporal order, is in actuality an extrapolation of the temporal order beyond the "now" of the actor's present. Nevertheless, for the Hobbesian actor, "the temporal order, which is the order of known events at a location, extends only up to the observer's 'now' and there it has a terminus." (4:320)

The Hobbesian actor cannot escape certain epistemological difficulties with cognized time. He knows the directly experienced, concrete events of the present, and he has noted the experienced events of the past as the facts of memory. He knows them in a dual mode —their relational sequence and their material content. While he may anticipate possibilities of the future in a projected temporal order, it is all induction. He cannot, through the necessities of inductive logic alone, know both a relationship between unknown events and the content of those events in a future time. What, then, for the Hobbesian prudent as actor?

His only interest in the physical states of two different times is an interest in what this means for his acting as a causal agent. Cause always signifies antecedence and consequence, the temporal order of relationship between events. With prudent action, however, there is always the reference of "a designe in hand" on the part of the actor. The material content of the events of future time, therefore, must be both regulable (conduced into a design) and regulated by the Hobbesian actor. His power to do so is his "present means to obtain some future apparent Good." (3:66) That is to say, regulative control may be available to the Hobbesian actor as the alternative to the impossibility of ascribing material content to the non-existent events of future time, for "things *to come* have no being at all" in Nature. (3:21)

Intentive Time

The cognized time of the Hobbesian actor has been categorized by Toda as that notion of time, older than the notion of spatialized time, in which time is "an indispensable component of our cognitive system." (6:374) It is a notion in which time is intentive. Toda places its source in "timing behavior" or the behavior associated with the timing of action, a "most basic" of animal behavior. It is behavior that involves both the freezing (action waiting) and the activation (action release) operations of a cognitive system. It is in this way that actions are subject to the pre-emptive regulation of cognition.

In the case of the present of behavior, as distinct from the past and the future, a "spatialized version" of time is introduced to deal with the movement of objects in the "static, timeless system" that is the present of analysis. It is with intentive time, rather than with spatialized time, that a present is inserted between the past and the future. From an epistemological standpoint, Toda is at one with Hobbes that whatever exists in the real world—has a being in Nature, that is—must be in the present. (6:376) Past and future are meaningful to the actor only because of a cognitive system that seems to operate "under a normative rule that the 'future' events must be taken as modifiable but the 'past' events should be taken as fixed." (6:376) Cognitively, therefore, while the past is determined, the future is not. Consequently, the "Trayne of Regulated Thoughts" (3:20) of the Hobbesian prudent can lead from the present events cognized in time to the acts of a causal agent in a projected temporal order of events.

REFERENCES

1. Shepard, Paul—*Thinking Animals: Animals and the Development of Human Intelligence* (Viking, 1978).

2. Heidegger, Martin—*Being and Time* (Macquarrie, J. & Robinson, E. Transl., SCM Press, Ltd., London 1962).

3. Hobbes's *Leviathan*—(Rep. of ed. of 1651, Oxford University Press 1909, Imp. of 1929).

4. Denbigh, K.G., "The Objectivity, or Otherwise of the Present," in Fraser, J.T., Lawrence, N. and Park, D. (eds.), *The Study of Time III* (Springer-Verlag, 1978), p. 307, cited hereafter as *The Study of Time III: Proceedings of the Third Conference of the International Society for the Study of Time* (Springer-Verlag, N.Y. 1978) pp. 370-388.

5. Ponty, J. Merleau, "Ideas of Beginnings and Endings in Cosmology" in *The Study of Time III*, p. 333.

6. Toda, M., "The Boundaries of the Notion of Time", in Fraser, J.T., Lawrence, N., and Park, D. (eds.) *The Study of Time III*, pp. 370-388.

7. Chasis, Herbert and Goldring, William (eds.)—*Homer William Smith: His Scientific and Literary Achievements* (New York University Press 1965)

CHAPTER XIII

The Future as Hobbesian Prudence

The Past as Powerlessness

So far as the future is concerned, the Hobbesian actor is severely constrained by the materiality of his own thought. Hobbes had given thought an exclusively material fundament. Nevertheless, the Hobbesian actor is caught up by the very non-materiality of the future. Nor is the past of any help here; because the past, too, has been reduced to non-materiality by Hobbes. If the past is only memory for the Hobbesian actor, the past then exemplifies only the nonduration of a particular configuration of materiality and the events associated with it.

The past can no longer be known as sensory cognition because it has been de-materialized. The future cannot yet be known as sensory cognition because it has still to materialize. Thought as materiality—the sensory cognition of representation and appearance—is unable to cognize a constitutive reality other than that which exists as a present material actuality. Again, so far as the future is concerned, the Hobbesian actor is left with consciousness, but without a cognizable actuality. The future is indeed as Hobbes put it—"A Fiction of the Mind"—absent its cognizability through thought.

What then is left to the Hobbesian actor to deal with the future? Nothing that is constitutive of the future. Only that which is regulative with respect to the future. The Hobbesian actor is left with a regulative duality. The future for the Hobbesian actor can only come into constitutive existence through the employment of that regulative duality. The one strand of the regulative duality is the regulative principle of causality. It is the logos of the order of things in the world for action. It is the regulative principle of cause and effect, antecedent and consequence in the world that is both anterior to and exterior to the potential actor. The other strand of the regulative duality is the principle of "regulated thought." It is the logos of the "Trayn" of thoughts of the agent of action; that sagacity with respect to "desire and designe," which is the world of action preferences within the Hobbesian actor.

The Hobbesian actor is left with only two fundamentals as starting points. The first is consciousness. The second is a logos—a regulating principle—both in his 'thought' and in 'the world for action.' Each of these is an outcome of the fundament of materiality on which the Hobbesian actor builds in time. But the very materiality of consciousness on the part of the Hobbesian actor is what cuts him off from time. By making the past "pure memory," he has reduced it to a "radical powerlessness." (1:181)

The past is powerless as memory, because as memory it has been detached from the sensory base of cognition and thereby stripped of its utility. The Hobbesian actor is always rooted in the sensory perceptions of present materiality, or the field of cognition circumscribed by present circumstances. The past is a perception that no longer exists as a representation, and so it is separated from the logos of the order of things in the world for action.

The Past As Consciousness

Nevertheless, the past as a memory without an image—as "pure memory"—exists for the Hobbesian actor as a subjective state, because memory of the past is inextricably woven into the personal existence of the Hobbesian actor. Personal existence, however, is detached from logos—from any regulative principle. For Hobbesian actors, personal existence is enmeshed "in the search of the causes of their own good and evill fortune." (2:82)

The past as "pure memory" consists of no more than "an original moment of (the actor's) history." (1:91)

Consciousness of personal existence is the actor's personal history in the attainment of the objects of desire, in assuring the way for the attainment of future desires, and in securing one's self against feared evils. The Hobbesian actor exists "in a perpetuall solicitude of the time to come." (2:82) The past as "pure memory" for the Hobbesian actor is "radically powerless" in relation to ordering the present for some future advantage. Still, that past provides the Hobbesian actor with a consciousness of the "Felicity" of his condition—or the progress of the actor in his desires—in terms of some continuity over time in both the "procuring . . . (and) the assuring of a contented life." (2:75)

Nonetheless, the Hobbesian actor is a realist and only a realist. "For realism, in fact, the invariable order of the phenomena of nature lies in a cause distinct from our perceptions, whether this cause must remain unknowable, or whether we can reach it by an effort (always more or less arbitrary) of metaphysical construction." (1:73) The Hobbesian actor builds only on this fundament of "a cause distinct from our perceptions." In "*regulated* thought" there is only "a hunting out of the causes, of some effect, present or past; or of the effects, of some present or past cause." (2:20) Hence the past cannot be solely representationless pure memory or consciousness of existence as personal history.

The Past As Expectation

Nor is the past so confined for the Hobbesian actor, for the past is also the past experience of an actor. This experience is the experience of past actions—the actor as an agency whereby changes are effected in the things of the material universe. The past is then remembered perceptions which are "a part of things," and which express and measure the "power of action" on the part of the agent of action. (1:68) Remembrance, or the "calling to mind . . . of our former actions," as Hobbes put it, by which the events connected to actions are cognized, leads to the expectational foresight that is prudence. An apt characterization of prudence, to borrow from Bergson, is that it is "the recollection of earlier analogous intuitions." (1:70)

Bergson, in fact, was at one with Hobbes when he noted that present perception can be transformed into "an occasion for remembering," and that the remembered images which survive as the past images of memory have survived because of their utility. (1:70) The remembered images of the Hobbesian actor, though personal to the actor, are taken to be "signes" of that reality which is impersonal and external to the actor. Nevertheless, the "signes" of Hobbes never yield certainty enough about antecedent/consequent in events, whether in the past or in the future. Prudence, as experience, presumes both forwards and backwards in time. "As Prudence is a *Praesumption* of the *Future*, contracted from the *Experience* of time *Past*: so there is a praesumption of things Past taken from other things (not future but) past also." (2:22)

The Present As Actuality And Prefiguration

Only the present is not a presumption. The present is there—an actuality, "a being in nature" rather than in memory or in mental fictions. (2:21) The present is there as a duration of both consciousness and materiality, and in relation to which the Hobbesian actor has an indeterminate power as an agent of action. That power is the power of "present means to obtain some future apparent Good." (2:66) The utility of prudence is always its utility as a perception of the past (as its utility) for the determination of the future:

> Nature has invented a mechanism for canalizing our attention in the direction of the future, in order to turn it away from the past—I mean of that part of our history which does not concern our present actions,—in order to bring to it at most, in the form of 'memories,' one simplification or another of anterior experience, destined to complete the experience of the moment; it is in this that the function of the brain consists. (3:181)

The present as a power of action involves both a consciousness of present circumstances and a regulative principle or logos of thought and action. Consciousness of present circumstances is a utilitarian consciousness of the efficacy of possible action: Efficacy, in turn, is based on present perceptions or perceived realities of the material universe for action. This material universe represents in varying degrees, "an action which we can accomplish upon things or which we must experience from them." (1:185) The link between present perception and impending action is such that "the present is idea-matter," and perception "a system of nascent acts, and the prefiguring of action in perception infuses perception with the actuality of activity." (1:74-75) In sum, for the Hobbesian actor, regulated thought "is an instrument of action, and not of representation." (1:83)

The Psychologizing Of Time

The action of the Hobbesian actor is always in the context of the event antecedent to the consequent, and of the consequent that is the sequal to the observed antecedent. Because of its particular presupposition of causality in the material world of exteriority, the Hobbesian actor really acts in terms of a projection of psychological time, and is able to visualize a reversal of the direction of time—Antecedent⇌Consequent—as part of the mental calculation of the effects of present action in terms of the preceding and succeeding sequels of action. The Hobbesian actor has merged physical time into psychological time. He has assigned to the development of the world of material exteriority the projective direction of psychological time. He is thereby able to schematize a succession of events along an axis that is a flow of time.

The Perceptual Consciousness of Prudence

Action by the Hobbesian actor that is a derivative of a "Trayn of regulated Thoughts" is possible because a transition between inner and outer experience is possible. It is possible as real experience possessing duration because it is tied to "the real structure of concrete magic" and does not "overstep the horizon of consciousness." (4:198) Prudence is a concept of inner experience derived from the actor's experience with the outer world of materiality. For prudence, the outer world is the perceptual field for real experience with the magic contents of real surroundings, or "the perceptual field of the content of consciousness." (4:198) The sensory fundament of thought for the Hobbesian actor—whereby "a man can have no thought, representing anything, not subject to sense" (2:23)—limited real experience to perceptual consciousness of the structures of material actuality, and constrained that consciousness to finiteness, to locus, to determinate magnitude, and to appearance.

While the material world of exteriority enters into the Hobbesian actor through the sensory organs, the Hobbesian actor intrudes inner processes of consciousness and thinking into the external world through the concept of causality as agency—the power of an actor with present means. Causality as agent must have its effect on perception, making it more than just conscious representation of the images of external things, whereas otherwise perception would never become a part of the acting agent. The Hobbesian actor is a conscious center of action. The perception of the acting agent as actor "expresses and measures the power of action in the living being. The indetermination of the movement or of the action which will follow the receipt of the stimulus . . . Perception, in its pure state, is then, in very truth, a part of things." (1:68)

The Being Of The Present

It was clear to Hobbes that experience always ends up in conjecture, whether projecting into future causality or retrospecting into the causality of past events. The present, however, was not the domain of experience. "The present *onely* has a being in nature," wrote Hobbes. This *being of the present* is taken to be an actuality. This *being of the present* consists of unique moments of duration in the structure of a perceptually sectioned portion of the material world, and with relation to which the felt state of sensation and movement on the part of the agent of action is the actual state in which lies the actuality of the present. (1:178) This *being of the present* is a psychologically defined present as that which is, because it is that which exists as "present means, to obtain some future apparent Good." (2:66) The Hobbesian actor has not only injected psychological time into the "real surroundings given in consciousness as a real image," (4:198); he has also attributed psychological duration to the duration of the phenomena of the world of material exteriority. Yet a psychologized actuality as consciousness of present reality places the Hobbesian actor in the context of a materiality without present duration in perception, for only "an ideal present—a pure conception, (is) the indivisible limit which separates past from future." (1:176) The context of materiality is real enough, nevertheless, to exist in consciousness as the perceptual fundament for those actions by which an undetermined future apparent good is to be realized.

The Future As Desire

Desire, with its object transcendent quality, precedes the future. That is to say, desire precedes that which is calculated to be an existant. What is desired by desire is to bring the desired preexistant into material existence. The future as to-be-existants is a not yet experienced reckoning of regulated thought, but the future is always subject to strict causality. Desire can only regulate the consciousness of an actor, but not an actuality of experience.

The future, since it lies outside the perceptual horizon, is conceivable only in thought. It is not conceivable as experience, for the reality of experience is given in the actualities of the perceptual field of consciousness. But the Hobbesian actor, because of the materiality of thought, cannot even know the future in thought. The future for the Hobbesian actor is always a fiction of the mind. The causality of the Hobbesian actor is an introspective aspect of experience which need only be psychologically adequate for action. The world of exteriority as the world for action is anterior to and external to the actor, and its causality does not have an introspective starting point.

The Hobbesian future, despite the *sagacitas* of "designe," is always absent the perceptual reality on which action will be based. Moreover, there is always the discrepancy between the time of causality in the world for action and the psychological time of the acting agent of causality. Present means as a power of an agent of action becomes, for the Hobbesian actor, a material reality with a potential relation to the world for action. Its potentiality is not just the potentiality of a sequence of events that satisfies the psychological time conditions of antecedent/consequent. It is also what is in waiting as potential "good and evil fortune" for the Hobbesian actor. In its temporal dimension as the future, the world for action can be represented but not experienced.

For the Hobbesian prudent, the future is egocentric and possessory. "Desire is by definition egocentric: it tends toward possession." (5:231) The normative concepts of Good and Evil are reduced to manipulative norms for reckoning. On the one hand, things—objects—are separable from rules of Good and Evil. On the other hand, "Things cannot be separated from the techniques which permit us to manipulate them." (5:136) The future is something that involves reckoning about a world of material exteriority. Reckoning—the techniques for manipulating choice—makes the future something that precipitates for the actor a present liberty of choice either to act or not to act. It is a choice for which there is no pre-emptive regulator. The future is not something that involves either reason forward or reason backward. What is it that bars the presence of a pre-emptive regulator for desire?

> What stands in our way is a rigid and over-simplified notion of objective reality, conceived as existing simply for recognition and as having no need of us whatsoever. (5:46-47)

The Hobbesian actor acts upon "a world of elements acting upon one another." (5:137) The world does not act upon the Hobbesian actor except to move him to act upon it. The Hobbesian world for action exists as a place of opportunity for an acting agent as an efficient cause. The world for action is known from the particular point of view of the actor. In terms of efficient cause, his acts are significant for what they produce. His sensibilization keeps him in the present of sensibility, but he imagines the future. His imagination of the future is in terms both of the cause of an imagined effect and a possessory stance about the future. The latter is an imagination about the future whereby the Hobbesian actor imagines what can accrue to him if he were but to have "any thing whatsoever" in his possession to do with it as he would.

The "uncertainty of signes" is the uncertainty of diverse things external to the Hobbesian actor. There is also, however, an uncertainty within him. It is the uncertainty attending the exercise of volition. This internal uncertainty of volition is not just an analytic uncertainty about the external signes. Designe imagines and imagination conduces to designe, but of what might be done the actor may be of a mixed and vacillating attitude about the doing of the thing.

The premise of incessant change underlies all thought of the Hobbesian actor. That premise is there as a pre-analytic comprehension. It is a comprehension not just of the world for action, but also of himself as actor, underlying that "continuall mutation" of his own constitution as a material body. The attainment of any particular desire at any specific time still leaves the actor in an unstable state with respect to imagined future change. No desire can be an ultimate end in the face of continual change. For the Hobbesian actor, there is neither "utmost ayme" nor "greatest good," (2:75) which leaves only that "progresse of the desire" in time whereby the Hobbesian actor can use "Felicity" as a measure of the fancies and judgments by which he has applied his "present means to obtain some future apparent Good." (2:66)

The future is both thought and action. The Hobbesian actor as thinker puts to one side the thought that action generates the situations of present life; that actions place persons *in situ*. Action is *a*-historical in all respects other than egocentric consciousness of the progress of desire in time. Action is a matter of the power of present means. It is not only that the past is psychologized as the empirics of memory. It is that the past is also psychologized as the empirics of experiential knowing. But that prudential knowing is the knowing only of the things of the world of material exteriority which have been represented as actual images. It is never an experiential knowing in which there is a knowing of the acting person in his subjectness. It is always a knowing in which the prudence that is experiential is confined to enhancing the efficiency of the Hobbesian actor as a causal agent of action.

REFERENCES

1. Bergson, Henri—*Matter and Memory* (Allen and Unwin, 1911)
2. *Hobbes's Leviathan*—(Rep. of ed. of 1651, Oxford University Press 1909, Imp. of 1929)
3. Bergson, Henri—*The Creative Mind* (Philosophical Library, 1946)
4. Pflug, Gunther "Inner Time and the Relativity of Motion" in Gunter, P.A.Y. (ed.)—*Bergson and the Evolution of Physics* (University of Tennessee Press, 1969)
5. Marcel, Gabriel—*Presence and Immortality* (M.A. Marcado, Transl., Duquesne University Press 1967)

CHAPTER XIV

The Future as Aristotelian Prudence

FOR THE HOBBESIAN ACTOR, the future as prudence begins and ends in materiality. For the Aristotelian actor, it neither begins nor ends in materiality. But materiality is there—unequivocally there—even though it is not a materiality identical with that of the Hobbesian actor.

The Transformation Of Desire Into Thought

The Aristotelian summation of prudence is cryptic: prudence is both desire that reasons and reason that desires. Desire is rooted in materiality, the materiality of sensation. Desire is a "motive cause" of action, the action that is directed to the end that is desired. (2:151) The things apprehended through sensation are either pleasant or painful. The attendant feelings of pleasure or pain lead to the actions of pursuit or avoidance. (2:141) The sensation of things present are present sensations. The affirmance of the pleasant or the painful in sensation moves action toward pursuit or avoidance in relation to the objects of sensation.

However, sensations are never experienced as sensations but as "simple assertion or simple apprehension by thought." (2:141) The Aristotelian meaning is that thought imposes on the materiality of sensation a particular form as a mental image. Therefore, "in the region of sense the objects of pursuit and avoidance have been defined for it." (2:143) The things of action are at one and the same time both objects of sensation and objects of cognition. Action is always directed to an end, the end being the object of desire. Thought enters into action because the object of desire is the point at which thought starts. (2:151)

The Future As Thought

It is intellect and not sensibility that introduced time into action. The action on the basis of sensibility is present action. Action in the present is the activity of engagement in actual pursuit or avoidance in relation to that which exists in actuality as a present sensibility. Intellect, however, can refer either to the past or to the future. The future becomes thought in terms of mental images. Time can be thought as "a divisible or indivisible unit," (2:137), and "the act of thought and the time required for the act are divisible." (2:139) It is thought, substituting mental images for the objects of sensation, that moves the Aristotelian actor to the action for which he has calculated as though he had the objects before him. Thus it is that the actor "deliberate(s) about the future in the light of the present." (2:143)

The pursuit and avoidance in thought is the equivalent of the pleasant and the painful of present sensation. "For mental images are like present sensations, except that they are immaterial." (2:145) Mental images, however, are not the decaying sense images of imagination, as they are for the Hobbesian actor. Imagination, for the Aristotelian actor, involves notions that are distinct from the affirmation of pursuit and the negation of avoidance.

The Future As Imagination

As against the present of sensibility, the future is always the product of imagination. "Now imagination may be rational or it may be imagination of sense." (2:155) The difference between the two is that the former is deliberative while the latter is not. The "deliberative imagination" of the Aristotelian actor is a particular form of imagination. It is "that form of imagination which comes from inference." (2:155)

The Future As Practical Intellect

The thought that enters into the end desired through action is "the practical intellect," which is the intelligence by which the means to an end is calculated. It is with the practical intellect that reason desires ("for rational wish is appetancy") and desire reasons ("when anyone is moved in accordance with reason, he is also moved according to rational wish"). (2:151) Still, the interaction of the two can leave the Aristotelian actor battling with contradictories within himself. It is only because thought cognizes time and its divisibility that desire (the optative) and intellect can be contradictory and in opposition to one another.

> For intelligence bids us resist because of the future, while appetite has regard only to the immediate present; for the pleasure of the moment appears absolutely pleasurable and absolutely good because we do not see the future. (2:153)

The Aristotelian actor has within himself the "motive causes" by which he can bring about some desired end of action involving the use of rational powers. The practical science and the theoretical science are differentiated in the thinking of the Aristotelian actor. The former is subordinated to desire, while the latter is not. The significance of this subordination is that "in practical sciences the principle of *action* is in the doer, and this is *choice*; for that which is done and that which is *chosen* are the same thing." (1:102 BKE) Practical action and the practical intellect and the "formula", or the principle of knowledge that is the reason constituent of the potency of practical action, are in the Aristotelian actor.

However, the rational powers of the Aristotelian actor—the

capability or potency with the reason that is knowledge—are not under necessity as respects their cause and effect. There must be something decisive in rational action if contradictory effects are to be avoided. What is decisive in practical action in accordance with reason as a principle of knowledge was put by Aristotle as follows:

> So in the case of the rational potencies there must be something else which decides, [against the simultaneous production of contradictory effects] and by this I mean desire or *choice*. For whichever of two things an animal desires by decision this it will bring about when it has the potency to do so and approaches that which can be acted upon. Thus, everything which is capable according to formula must act on that which it desires, whenever it desires that of which it has the capability and in the manner in which it has that capability. . . . And to add the further specification "if nothing external prevents" is no longer needed; for the agent has the potency in the manner in which this is a potency of acting, and the potency is such not in any way whatsoever but in a certain way which also takes care of the external hindrances, since these are barred by some of the specifications present. (1:151 Bk Ⓗ)

If all that is possible is the apparent good that is the outcome of the practical action of the practical intellect, then the future of the Aristotelian actor is still without a pre-emptive regulator. The question of a pre-emptive regulator of the ends of action bears upon the activity of both the Hobbesian and the Aristotelian actors. It is non-existent in the case of the former. Is it existent in the case of the Aristotelian actor? The apparent good is always a "practical good" that is always a "something which may not be good under all circumstances." (2:151) Apparent good is necessarily a contingent good and cannot be a pre-emptive regulator of action. The apparent good of practical action is an end that lies outside the action itself and imposes a limit on that action. (1:152 Bk Ⓗ) As to these ends of practical action, the motive causes of practical action cannot be a pre-emptive regulator. Nevertheless, with respect to ends, performance in and of itself is taken to be an end, for it is through performance that matter as potentiality is tranformed into an actuality, so that it possesses a particular form. (1:155 Bk⊕)

Here the motive causes of practical action would function as a directive intelligence. Desire and aversion signify a directionality of activity or endeavor toward or from something on the part of an actor. Materiality and the attributes of sense provide an actor with a directive (or directional) intelligence by which to begin voluntary action. However, directive intelligence is not the regulative intelligence of a pre-emptive regulator of the ends of action. The future remains without a pre-emptive regulator, existing only as a possessory state.

Aristotelian And Hobbesian Materiality

For the Aristotelian actor, sensibility cannot exhaust the meaning of materiality. For the Aristotelian actor, the practical intellect cannot exhaust the meaning of reason. For the Aristotelian actor, the actor does not exist simply as the materiality of another body of nature.

The Hobbesian actor, in contrast to the Aristotelian actor, exists only as an embodiment of materiality. The actions of the Hobbesian actor are explicable only in the terms of such an embodiment. There is nothing about the Hobbesian actor that exists besides his own materiality. Whatever he is or does can be attributed to this materiality. The Hobbesian actor as subject exists as the repository of the attributes of materiality. The attributes of materiality are taken to be the attributes of existing as a person.

His actuality or his substance is his materiality, for the sensibles of that materiality are its function. Sensation becomes thought, although it is accepted by the Hobbesian actor that sensible appearances are imagic fancies. It is enough to explain sensation by the materiality of objects and their relation to the sense organs. For the Aristotelian, however, Being exists prior to sensation, "for a sensation is surely not a sensation of itself." (1:68 Bk Γ) Moreover, appearance—as distinct from sensation—requires a subject for action and appearance does more than just exist.

The Hobbesian actor, in consequence of his materiality is always lacking in quiddity or essence. He is a material embodiment of matter. In this embodiment he exists "in an underlying subject as in matter." (1:127 Bk Z) To which Aristotle added: "But things which exist as matter, or which include matter, are not the same as their essence." As to what matter meant, he explained, "By matter I mean that which in itself is not stated as being the whatness of something, nor quantity, nor any of the other senses of 'being'." (1:110 Bk Z) So the Hobbesian actor, in all his materiality, although a sensible existant, is without "the essence of a man." (1:140 Bk H) He is without that compositeness of form and matter, where the essence that is the individual "whatness" belongs to the form or actuality which does not exist apart from man's sensible corporeality. (1:125 Bk Z)

Materialism, for the Hobbesian actor, restricts the significance of sensations. Through this restriction on sensations it restricts the significance of action for the Hobbesian actor. Sensations are part of a kinetic theory of matter. Sensations are either representative sensations or affective sensations. Representative sensations are always present appearances of the properties of objects that are external to the actor. These properties are always the sensible qualitites of the objects that cause them. What the objects are is one thing. What their images, or representations or appearances are, is another. The after-effect of representative sensations are images. The prudence of the Hobbesian actor is therefore limited to the corrective function of experience in relation to directive intelligence.

For the Hobbesian actor, desire and aversion require a less contingent ground for action than that provided to thought by decaying sensory images. Hobbesian imagination consists of a "decaying sense" of the appearance of external things. Representative sensations, being sensations of present time and present place, decay into impressions, because "other objects more present succeeding, and working on us the Imagination of the past is obscured and made weak." (3:14) Hobbesian imagination consists of that which, though once apparent to sense, has lost its sensory dominance as a present appearance of something external.

The present is always a time/place present of a sensible embodiment impinged upon by the motion of other bodies in space. Materiality as sensation is the expression of a primary way of Being. The present as materiality in time/place has sensation as its primary way of Being. Representative sensations as the sensible qualities of time/place do more than define the duration of materiality as the present. They equate materiality with Being, even while the "cause of sense" and the "qualities called sensible" are taken to exist in the objects that are external to the actor. (3:11) The Hobbesian assertion that it is only the present that "has a being in Nature" sums it up for the Hobbesian actor.

Eductive Representations: The Aristotelian Imagination

The Aristotelian actor, however, recognizes more than representative sensations. The more that is recognized by the Aristotelian actor consists of eductive representations. One mode of eductive representations is the Aristotelian imagination. The Aristotelian imagination includes that which is excluded from the imagination of the Hobbesian actor. The Aristotelian imagination is not on the same footing as sense perception.

The Aristotelian "imagination is the faculty in virtue of which we say that an image presents itself to us." (2:125) The images of imagination are not dependent upon sensations, and hence are not of necessity representative. "Imaginings prove for the most part false." (2:125) Imagination is different from the sense perception that it presupposes, and it is different from the judgments of intellect or thought. The Aristotelian imagination can occur as a mental presentation, and the images of such presentation need not be the representative sensations of an objective reality. The Aristotelian imagination encompasses eductive representation.

The Future As Pre-formation

Eductive representations open for the Aristotelian actor two possibilities that are denied the Hobbesian actor. Both of these possibilities are related in that—to use Heidegger's term—they each bear on the "pre-formation" of the future. It is possible for the presentations of Aristotelian imagination to be free of those time/place constraints of representative sensations by which the present of sensibility is defined. The "now" of the representations of sensibility is not at the core of eductive representations. Absent this core, eductive representations permit another kind of unity between the present, the past, and the future. It is not that externally defined "now" of sensibly materialized actuality in a successive sequence of the "nows" of sense representation.

The Aristotelian "Being" that is excluded by the materialism of the Hobbesian actor opens the way to a different framework for action in time. Materialism without Being excludes the possibility of subjectivity on the part of an actor. There is the consciousness of the sensibility caused by external objects, but not subjectivity. The Hobbesian actor as another body in nature, and functioning like those bodies as part of a kinematic theory of matter, knows himself only in terms of an external indicator of his effectiveness as an efficient cause. He measures this effectiveness by the standard of Felicity, which is the measure of progress in the attainment of desire.

The eductive representations of the Aristotelian imagination, as an aspect of the quiddity or essence of Being, and by virtue of which "an image presents itself," infuses action with a different relation to the past, present and future. The Aristotelian actor can act with reference to what Heidegger explained as "presencing, letting-be-present: presence." (4:10) For the Aristotelian actor the "now" of the sensory present materiality may have the meaning of an "unconcealing" or "allowing-to-presence." The temporal present is always "a kind of approach and bringing about." There is a "coming toward" in the "allowing-to-presence" or unconcealing of that which is not yet present. (4:10-12)

> Approaching, being not yet present, at the same time gives and brings about what is no longer present, the past, and conversely what has been offers future to itself. The reciprocal relation of both at the same time gives and brings about the present. (4:13)

145

This kind of pre-formation of the future is not acceptable to the Hobbesian actor, for it violates the inescapable time/place finiteness of sensory knowing. Nothing can be imagined except that which has first been perceived by the organs of sense, including the brain and nerves as sensory organs. (3:14-15) The future cannot be imagined, but can be only "a fiction of the mind." (3:21) The future is to be thought of in terms of applying a sequence or pattern of past actions to present acts. The future as event is nothing more than expectation, the uncertainty of which is diminished by the experience of the actor. (3:21) The world of the Hobbesian actor is one of "pure exteriority, a world of elements acting on one another." (5:137) The world of "pure exteriority" is one about which the Hobbesian actor searches for what effects can be produced through the power of his present actions. Thought is regulated so as to know the things of that world in terms of what can be done with them. Hobbesian actors inquire only into "the causes of their own good and evil fortune." (3:82) There can be no pre-formation of the future for Hobbesian actors.

Kinematic and Kinetic Materiality

The Hobbesian actor has less a theory of matter than a theory of finite (place, magnitude, time) sensory cognition that is the ground for acting as efficient cause under conditions in which the kinematics of matter provides the actor with more or less uncertain "signes" of events antecedent or consequent in an unknown chain of external causality. The Aristotelian actor has a theory of matter. Where the materialism of the Hobbesian actor is kinematic, the materialism of the Aristotelian actor is kinetic. The materialism of the former views the motion of matter apart from its causes, some of which may become known to prudence through the searchings of "signes" uncertain. The materialism of the latter views matter as containing its own potentiality. The kinetic materialism of the Aristotelian actor provides a further cognitive fundament to the pre-formation of the future.

Matter simply as materiality is characterized by its indeterminateness. It is absent the particularity that makes it a something, a definable particularity that would give it subjectness. For a material to become something in particular — to lose its indeterminateness — lies in the potentiality of matter. The potential of matter is what it can become as actuality. The source of this potential of becoming may be either outside of material things or within them. Where the source is external, matter becomes all that deliberately willed changes can bring about. Where the source is within material things, their potentiality of becoming is what they will be of themselves according to their own material principle.

Potentiality becomes actuality through attainment of the form by which matter loses its indeterminateness. However, actuality is prior to potentiality. It is prior in knowledge — "knowledge of that which is in *actuality* must be prior to the formula or knowledge of that which is potential." (1:154 Bk⊕) It is prior in generative requisites — "it is always by a thing in *actuality* that another thing becomes *actualized* from what it was *potentially*" (1:154 Bk⊕)

What is the relation of potentiality to pre-formation of the future? All potentiality is perishable. Potentiality exists for the sake of an end. As for its becoming actual, however, potentiality may either cease to be or come to exist actually. That it may possibly not exist, even though it is a potentiality that is capable of existing, establishes the destructibility of what exists potentially.

Potentiality as a power for actuality is subject to a pre-emptive regulator, "for that which has the capability of not existing may not be; and that which may not be is destructible, either without qualification, or with respect to that which it may not be." (1:156 H) The indwelling principle of potentiality portends a pre-formation of the future. But material things exist under conditions of regulative choice that can selectively permit or prevent the fulfillment of potentiality as actuality. The world is not one of "pure exteriority," one where no actor enters into the pre-formation of the future. For the Aristotelian actor, thought and choice function as a cause in the generation of things.

REFERENCES

1. *Aristotle's Metaphysics*—(Hippocrates G. Apostle, Transl. and Comm., Indiana University Press, 1966)
2. Aristotle *DeAnima*—(Hicks, R.D., Transl., Introductory Notes, Cambridge University Press 1907)
3. *Hobbes's Leviathan*—(Rep. of ed. of 1651, Oxford University Press 1909, Imp. of 1929)
4. Heidegger, Martin *On Time and Being*—(Joan Stambaugh Transl., Harper & Row 1972)
5. Marcel, Gabriel *Presence and Immortality*—(M.A. Marcado, Transl., Duquesne University Press 1967)

CHAPTER XV

The Times of Time

Heterogenic and Homogenic Time

ARISTOTLE CONCEPTUALIZED TIME as that within which everything takes place. Nevertheless, the time that is conceptualized as so universally inclusive also has its less inclusive times. Indeed, it is the times of time that are critical for the futures of prudence. The Hobbesian prudent, for example, has no concept of time, but of timing. Volitional time is the prudential knowing of time. Volitional time is the time of opportunity. True enough, signs antecedent and signs consequent appear as a sequence in time. It is not this that is volitional time. It is time as the manifestation of possible causal connectivity between the appearance of things and is part of sensibilization and sensibilized thought. What infuses the times of time into time itself are designe and prudence.

What is the fundament on which prudence relates itself to time? An agent of action—an efficient cause—must encapsulate time into the causal effectiveness of his agency. Time can be cognized as heterogenic, in its temporality, but an acting agent in terms of his agency, must transform this temporal heterogeneity into an experienced homogeneity of time. That which is neither physical nor spatial must be transformed into the timing of action. That which is neither before nor after must be made the object of a "distinction between the past and the future divided by the present." (1:376)

The homogeneity of time is the time experienced as "normal

time." What is taken to be "normal time" is "event-investigating time." (1:385) Prudence is focused on time as a condition under which prudence judges that the agent of action will have sufficient control of a future event. Prudence as much experience, and much experience as memory, still cannot put time into an "oscillating" mode; that is, force that which has happened as a perceived, memorized and learned event to retrace itself.

> The exact duplication of the repeated processes, however, is a determinism. What if there is a quantum or two miserasure in someone's memory? That may create precognitions and prophecies. And precognitions and prophecies are, in contrast to the second dimension of time, (oscillating time) well within the range of our stretched imagination of time. (1:386-87)

Event Time

Hobbesian prudence has no theory of nature's events in time. It is a prudence that is without any interest in time as part of a physical description of nature. It is so disinterested because of its avoidance of remote, ultimate and speculative causes that is itself part of its avoidance of overknowing. For the Hobbesian prudent, it is only the present—a conscious "now"—that has "a being in Nature." The past consists of "decaying sense" images. This sense based theory of time requires the decay of the images of sensibilization in order to characterize the past as the time past of sensibilized occurrences. The Hobbesian present has its roots in the Augustinian concept of time.

> Present is in the full sense of the word, past and future are and are not, they are some sort of non-being, or half-being. The main point in Augustine's analysis seems to be this: The experience of the present, he says, if it did not fall into the past would be eternity. The falling into the past of the present, which is time, is a sort of degeneration of eternity. (i.e., decay of eternity.) (2:340-41)

Hobbesian prudence is interested only in the "now" of the agency of action. The time of "now" is the time that comes into present existence with the occurrences of which the agent of action is aware. The future is not a mode of time in which one experiences. Nevertheless, the "now" that is the present for the Hobbesian prudent is more than a point in linear time. Straightforwardly put, time is "a relational characteristic of events—including those events in the brain and in conscious awareness which provide the sense of a 'present'. " (3:323) Time is adapted to the phenomena existing at the level of conscious awareness.

The event relational time sense of Hobbesian prudence is locked into a particular structure of events. It is the event structure for the maintenance of that which one has gained as contingent on the next acquisition, and the event structure necessary because of the general and restless inclination for power after power. It is, in short, the event structure of felicity. There exists, therefore, a reference in consciousness for action with directionality over time. The consciousness of Hobbesian prudence encompasses both awareness and experience, not only of a pattern of relational causation, but also of opportunity for event relational causality. The experience of prudence supplies the epistemology for retrospective cognition. What is missing is the epistemology for acting prospectively. Volitional time as the time of opportunity is cognized in terms of the practicalities of the time of teleological choice. As to this volitional time as a point of choice in time, Turner, drawing upon Aristotle's concept of poesis, has written

> . . . that when time is genuinely poietic or creative, the present moment is not a point or dividing-line with no temporal thickness; rather it is a region, a specious present, which contains a field of undetermined possibilities and within which a pure teleology, governed only by the will of the individual, can operate. And now we have an explanation for the curious phenomenon that is obvious to all of us, but inexplicable in analytical terms: Freedom. (4:627)

Social Time As Event Relational Time

Hobbesian prudence made relationality the essence of the power of an acting agent. It also made power itself an event producing or "event instigating" potency. The potency was succinctly put as the "present means whereby to obtain some future apparent Good." (5:66) Relationality between persons as containing a potency for event production leads to social time as one of the times of time. Social time is an event relational time. Social time, to use the terms of Gurvitch, is one of "the multiplicity of times," one of the times of time. (6:171) The relationality that is the essence of power as "event instigating" moves prudential thought and action into the divergent manifestations of social life and into different levels of social reality. Society, class and group as social structures endeavor to control the multiplicity of times in social time. Gurvitch, after enlarging on the importance of realizing that social structures exist "in specific graduations of times," went on to provide a classification of eight kinds of social time.

1. *The time of long duration and slow motion* where the past is projected into the present and future.
2. A second sort is the *deceptive time* which under the appearance of long duration and slow motion hides potentialities of sudden and unexpected crises.
3. Third, I shall mention the *time of irregular cycles between* the appearance and disappearance of rhythms—these enigic series of intervals and moments intervening between the durations.
4. The fourth is *cyclical time*, whose apparent headlong rush masks a refolding upon itself (so that no actual advancement is made); the past, present, and future are projected mutually one into the other—which leads to an emphasis upon their continuity and to the weakening of contingency, while the qualitative element of this time is, on the contrary, brought into prominence.
5. We now arrive at the fifth kind of social time which I suggest has to be distinguished for the purpose of sociological analysis. This is *the time remaining behind itself* or, expressed otherwise, the time whose moments are too long delayed, despite the future which it actualizes in the present without, however, making it effective.
6. Sixth, we may point out a *time alternating between advance* and backwardness where the actualizations of the past and future into the present are in competition.
7. As a seventh kind I will mention what I shall call *time in advance*

of itself. In this kind of time the continuous, the contingent, and the qualitative triumph together over their opposites.
8. Finally, as the eighth and last kind I shall point out *explosive time*, which dissolves the present as well as the past in the creation of the future Immediately transcended. (6:175-78)

The order of things of Aristotelian prudence brings to the fore a different set of questions than the event temporality of before and after, which is the antecedent and consequent ordering of event appearance in Hobbesian prudence. Assume, for example, an A and B-series of events.

The B-series has as its generating relation *earlier* (or *later*) *than* (alternatively *before* or *after*) and it thus represents a serial ordering which runs from earlier to later according to relations of precedence and subsequence. The A-series, by contrast, runs from past through present to future, and is a series in which events are not so much ordered as *determined*—determined, that is to say, by non-permanent decisions concerning their pastness, presentness or futurity. Although the same events never change their B-ordering, they do change their A-determinations; they change from being future, to present to past, according to what we call 'happening,' 'becoming,' or 'coming into being.' (7:150)

What is specially to be noted is how the A and B-series of events are combined in Hobbesian prudence. It has nothing to say about the causality of the B-series of events. Its say is restricted to the A-series of events, which is the basis of volitional time. "The decision that an event is past, present or future" is made "mind-dependent." (7:150) At the same time, it fuses into one the coming into being of things (only the present has a being in nature) with their appearance. It is a view of temporality that is compatible with the logical naturalism (or logical materialism) of Hobbesian prudence. Furthermore, volitional time, through the imposition of will and consciousness into temporality "implies the splitting of the present into future, present and past." (8:160) Designe, as consciousness, goes beyond perception, through imagination, and separates the future as realized desire from the present. Prudence, "as the temporal structure of our experience" (8:161) provides the knowledge of antecedent events about which the "wit" of judgment conceives the causal associations by which to choose causally generative action for the attainment of designe.

The Temporality Of An Order

Aristotelian prudence brings to the fore the temporality of an order of things. The time of an order of things is one of the times of time. An order is not something that is perceived as a sensible thing. An order is not known as the pictured or imagined present of an appearance. An order involves a duration that is not a perceptual duration. An order is not a serial event. The time of an order is not volitional time.

An order is the substratum of the existence of things. The duration of an order is to be understood as a temporal periodicity. Event relationality takes place in the temporal periodicity of an order. There is an arrow of time in the temporality of an order. This arrow of time is in the "coming-to-be and passing-away of things which by nature come-to-be and pass-away." (9:163)

The future as a succession of orders is the temporal periodicities attaching to successive orders of things. There are no voids between the coming-to-be and the passing-away of these orders. There is, in other words, no cessation in the coming-to-be "because the passing away of one thing is the coming-to-be of another thing, and the coming-to-be of one thing is the passing-away of another thing." (9:191) A double movement of contrary kinds is essential both for the unbroken continuity of coming-to-be and passing-away and "in order that there may not be only one change occurring." (9:135) The substratum of an order is matter. The substance of each order is in its materiality, which contains both a material causality that gives to things their physical distinctiveness, and a causality of form or "end in view" that defines their essential nature. The things of an order which, in their materiality, "can both *be* and *not be*" define the sphere in which must occur coming-to-be and passing-away. (9:309)

The future will always exist because there is no cessation in the coming-to-be of the order of things. The question put by Aristotelian prudence is "whether there is anything which will necessarily exist in the future." (9:321) The question was put by Aristotle because the observed sequence in time in which things appear without cessation raised considerations about what is necessary in coming-to-be between the prior and the posterior, and between the posterior and the prior. Aside from things which are eternal and absolutely necessary, the future will consist of things which are only conditionally necessary, and of things whose substance is imperishable. Conditional necessity introduces into the serial relationality of event instigation and volitional time the possibility of not coming-to-be between earlier and later events as members of a series.

An acting prudent introduces efficient cause into an order. In the materiality that is the substratum of an order, there is already material cause and the "end in view" causality of the form of matter. Moreover, efficient cause is introduced into a process of coming-to-be that is without cessation. An order of things within a "perpetual process" of nature exists in the temporal periodicity of its actuality as one of the times of the time by which change is reckoned. "If there is no time, neither can there be a *before* and an *after* in time." (10:202 Bk Λ) Through ceaseless coming to be, however, orders of things are tied into a whole that is an ultimate order, namely, the universe. The essence of the universe as substance or whatness is its coherence as a whole. "The continual coming-to-be of coming-to-be is the nearest approach to eternal being." (9:317) The succession of orders in time as material manifestations of coming-to-be is a succession of orders of coherence about actuality. The acquisition in time of the "greatest possible coherence" is cosmology forward. The coherence of any order is its matterless actuality, although the things of any order have matter. The future as orders of things is the temporal periodicities of both matter and matterless actuality.

Orderless Temporality

The Hobbesian world for action is not represented to the actor as a lawful order of things. No such order of the world for action can be a sensible representation. Nature is only the sensibilized finiteness of subjectively experienced phenomena. The Hobbesian actor never perceives nature as a unit, but he has an individual unity of experience about nature. The world for action is not a nature that contains any intrinsic principle. The sensibilization of the Hobbesian actor leaves the world for action without substance. There is nothing that has its own intrinsic nature. Sensibilization leaves the world for action with only antecedent and consequent. No idea or conception of nature is possible that has not been first reduced to perception, and thus reduced to the time, place and magnitude of sensibilization.

For the Hobbesian actor, the external world is the world whose horizon is bounded by the sensibly perceptual, so that both the perceptual images of the external world are the content of consciousness, and the experience of the actor with the external world is experience with the actualities of real images. It is in this sense that only the present as duration has a "Being in Nature" for the Hobbesian actor. The things of the external world are perceived from the utilitarian standpoint of regulated thought. The practical essence of the utilitarian interest of the Hobbesian actor in the external world imposes a perceptual point of view and subjugates the knowledge of consequences to desire.

For the Hobbesian actor, the external world of materiality, existing as it always does within the limits of sensibility and a perceptual horizon, can never be just a possibility of thought. Nor can experience, as the consciousness of actuality, be subjected to speculative concepts. All knowledge, including that of science—which "is the knowledge of Consequences, and dependence of one fact upon another"—is subordinated to its utility for action. The experientially known causality, including the manner of its causation, from a prior time provides that knowledge of the interdependence of fact which, "when like causes come into our power, we see how to make it produce the like effects." (5:37) The volitional time of an opportunity for action is a contingently experienced time of time.

The Time Of The Agent Of Action

Regulated thought limits the external world in thought, because the sensory fundament of its representation as objects makes actuality for the Hobbesian actor the fact of sense and memory. As a sensory actuality of fact it can exist in the perceptual consciousness of more than one person, who then "know it together," even though as between them as actors the objects of desire lack identicality or "similitude." Phenomena and the connections between them exist within a duration of time that is common to the consciousness of all actors. "All these consciousnesses, being human consciousnesses, seem to us to live in the same duration. Hence, all their outer experiences unfold in the same duration." (11:197)

There is a double sense in which the agent of action is located in time. There is, first, the materiality of the circumstances of one's being in time. There is, second, the materiality of the way of thinking on the part of the actor, which makes thought the materiality of the appearance of the external world of sensibility in time. Hobbes' "Trayn of Regulated Thoughts" or "The Discourse of the Mind" as he put it, introduces a certain gyroscopic quality to thought only because it is regulated by desire. What is desire, however, but the subjective state which attends the materialization of an imagined thing. Thought about sense knowable cause and effect is both the materiality of thought in time and the materiality in time of action as cause and consequence.

REFERENCES

1. Toda, M., "The Boundaries of the Notion of Time," in Fraser, J.T., Lawrence, N., and Park, D., (eds.)—*The Study of Time III: Proceedings of the Third*

Conference of the International Society for the Study of Time, (Springer-Verlag, N.Y. 1978), pp. 370-388.

2. Merleau-Ponty, J., "Ideas of Beginnings and Endings In Cosmology", in Fraser, J.T., Lawrence, N., and Park, D., (eds.)—*The Study of Time III: Proceedings of the Third Conference of the International Society for the Study of Time*, (Springer-Verlag, N.Y. 1978), pp. 333-350.

3. Denbigh, K.G. "The Objectivity, or Otherwise of the Present", in Fraser, J.T., Lawrence, N., and Park, D., (eds)—*The Study of Time III: Proceedings of the Third Conference of the International Society for the Study of Time*, (Springer-Verlag, N.Y. 1978), pp. 307-329.

4. Turner, F., "Poiesis: Time and Artistic Discourse," in Fraser, J.T., Lawrence, N., and Park, D. (eds.)—*The Study of Time III: Proceedings of the Third Conference of the International Society for the Study of Time*, (Springer-Verlag, N.Y. 1978), pp. 614-633.

5. Hobbes's *Leviathan*—(Rep. of ed. of 1651, Oxford University Press, 1909, Imp. of 1929).

6. Gurvitch, Georges, "Social Structure and the Multiplicity of Times," in Tiryakian, E.A., (ed.)—*Sociological Theory, Values, and Socio-Cultural Change* (Free Press, Glencoe 1963), pp. 171-184.
Gurvitch assigns credit for the origin of the concept of "social time" to the philosopher Henri Bergson in his work *Creative Evolution* (1907)

7. Denbigh, K.G., "In Defence of *the* Direction of Time", in Fraser, J.T., Haber, F.C., and Mueller, G.H. (eds.)—*The Study of Time, Proceedings of the First Conference of the International Society for the Study of Time*, (Springer-Verlag, N.Y. 1972), pp. 148-157.

8. Watanabe, Satosi, "Creative Time", in Fraser, J.T., Haber, F.C., and Mueller, G.H. (eds.)—*The Study of Time, Proceedings of the First Conference of the International Society for the Study of Time*, (Springer-Verlag, N.Y. 1972), pp. 159-189.

9. *Aristotle on Coming-To-Be and Passing-Away*—(E.S. Forster, Transl., Harvard University Press, 1955).

10. Aristotle's *Metaphysics*—(Hippocrates G. Apostle, Transl. and Comm., Indiana University Press, 1966).

11. Pflug, Gunter, "Inner Time and the Relativity of Motion", in Gunter, P.A.Y. (ed)—*Bergson and the Evolution of Physics* (University of Tennessee Press, 1969).

CHAPTER XVI

The Cosmology of Prudential Futures

Futures As Cosmology

Hobbesian prudence has evolved into the technologized strategizing that is now subsumed within the larger technical science of managing. More than did Aristotelian prudence, it fit well into what Heisenberg has described as

> an extremely rigid frame for natural science which formed not only science but also the general outlook of great masses of people. This frame was supported by the fundamental concepts of classical physics, space, time, matter and causality; the concept of reality applied to the things or events that we could perceive by our senses or that could be observed by means of the refined tools that technical science had provided. Matter was the primary reality. . . . Utility was the watch word of the time. (1:197)

The understanding of utilitarian pragmatics was clearly that the things of the world "consist of matter, and matter can produce and can be acted upon by forces." (1:196) Even the metaphysics of Kant had recognized force and action as derivatives of the connection that had been made by Hume between cause and effect. (2:5) Both philosophy and physics were joined in the primacy of the concept of causality, but not in "the concepts of mind, of the human soul or of life." (1:197)

The "designe" of the acting prudent (Hobbesian) is enframed in the concept of materialized reality. By its regulation of thought, "designe" made the substance of strategy another—or alternative—materialization of the world. Causal agency was the power whereby the acting prudent had power to produce matter from matter. Cosmoplastics refers to an independent and operative power by which a cosmos as a material order is originated and brought into being. It is in this sense that strategy is cosmoplastics.

Aristotelian as well as Hobbesian prudence each possess cosmoplastic potency with respect to a material order. It is this cosmoplastic potency for materialization that makes the futures of prudence, both cosmological and cosmogonic. The futures of prudence, that is to say, are the futures of a cosmos materialized as an order of existence. Cosmoplastics is the technologized gnostics of prudence. Strategy, therefore, is cosmogonic with respect to the future.

Futures As Cosmology Forward and Cosmology Backward

From cosmologic and cosmogonic standpoints, the difference between Aristotelian prudence, on the one hand, and Hobbesian prudence, on the other, is the difference between cosmology forward and cosmology backward. Hobbesian prudence has constrained and reduced thinking to a potency with respect to an object of thought. Aristotelian prudence has not so constrained and reduced thinking. For Aristotelian prudence, it is always that at its ultimate "Thinking is the thinking of Thinking." (3:209 Bk Λ) Being introduces "the thinking of Thinking" into prudential knowing.

How is it, none the less, that Aristotelian prudence may be characterized as cosmology forward, while Hobbesian prudence may only be characterized as cosmology backward? For one thing, simply to pick up Aristotle's own line of argument, if thinking were only a potency with respect to an object

> . . . it is clear that something else would be more honorable than the Intellect, namely, the object of thought; for to think or thinking

may belong even to that which thinks of the worst objects, so that if this is to be avoided (for there are even things which it is better not to see than to see), Thinking would not be the best of things. (3:209 Bk Λ)

Hobbesian Prudence: Cosmology Backward

The juncture of thinking as potency with respect to an object, together with the juncture of thinking as a calculative potency by which to extract from, and use up or assure, the possessory good of things for purposes of designe, leads Hobbesian thinking to the abandonment of that which it has once materialized as a future good. The abandonment is because of the loss of calculative potency in relation to that previous object as a possessory good. In the ceaseless search for felicity, Hobbesian prudence must ever return to the changing content of designe. Hobbesian prudence must ever return to designe as its own first cause and discover another potency with respect to other objects of desire. It is this that makes Hobbesian prudence cosmology backwards. It is in cosmology backward—the return to re-materialization of another beginning (first cause) of another cosmoplastics of a future—that there is the significance of Hobbesian felicity. The position of Hobbesian prudence is that felicity, as the progress of desire encountering the invisible causes of good and evil fortune, compels the Hobbesian actor ever to engage in further acquisitions in order to assure those already possessed. Cosmology backwards is another re-materialization of an event structure as the cosmoplastics of felicity.

Prudence and Wisdom

What bears also on the distinction between cosmology forward and cosmology backward is the relationship in Aristotelian prudence of prudence itself to wisdom. The two are separate, but linked. They are not so linked that one is subordinate to the other. "Prudence does not employ wisdom in her service, but provides means for the attainment of wisdom—does not rule it, but rules in its interests." (4:207)

What is wisdom as against prudence? Aristotle located wisdom in a place superior to that of science, and made wisdom a path to something beyond that attainable by prudence. The wise not only know the principles of reason underlying cognition, "but also the truth about those principles. Wisdom, therefore, will be the union of (intuitive) reason with (demonstrative) scientific knowledge." (4:190) What is constitutive about wisdom is that it is knowledge "about objects of the noblest nature." Wisdom, therefore, is not concerned with an end of action "in the sense of some realizable good," as is prudence. Wisdom does not take man as "the best of all things in the universe," and it is concerned with "other things of a far diviner nature then man." (4:190, 191-92)

Aristotelian Prudence: Cosmology Forward

It is through this relationship of prudence to wisdom that the futures of Aristotelian prudence may be characterized as cosmology forward. It is a prudential knowing that is not confined within the fence of deliberate under-knowing, which is a hallmark of Hobbesian prudence. The latter is fenced in by the exclusion of all that has not to do with the present power whereby to produce the future good, one that has taken shape in an imagined possession and that has been fortified by "designe". Hobbesian prudence, with its constrained result-oriented calculative knowing, shuts out all else, and forever turns its reasoning back upon those "practical affairs" that are the only objects of its concern. The knowing of the causality within the cosmos that lies behind the causes of events is limited to that which sensibilization discloses in the observation of events, and to the remembrance of these events in a particular sequence of antecedent and consequent, and, finally, to a "designe" regulated thinking about these events.

Through its linkage to wisdom, Aristotelian prudence searches for the knowing that passes beyond "ability to have sensations . . . common to all, and therefore easy, but not a mark of wisdom." Knowledge of that which underlies is universal knowledge, "and the most universal things are on the whole the hardest for men to know, for they are most removed from sensations." Moreover, Aristotelian prudence turns upon its own knowing of "what are the kinds of causes and principles whose science is wisdom." It is through this linkage of prudence to that which is "not a productive science," but a "science in order to understand"—that Aristotelian prudence enfolds cosmology forward into the science which is wisdom. (3:14-15 Bk A)

Prudential Good As Gnostics

Where, by comparison, Hobbesian prudence leaves the acting agent to respond to the material universe beyond the reach of sensibilization by anxiety and fear of fancied "Invisible Agents," Aristotelian prudence moves on into a further knowing.

> It is evident, then, that we must acquire *knowledge* of the first causes (for we say that we understand each thing when we think that we know its first cause), and causes are spoken of in four senses. In one sense, we say that *the substance* or the essence is a cause (for the *why* leads us back to the ultimate formula, and the first *why* is a cause and a principle); in another, it is the matter or the underlying subject; in a third, the source which begins the motion; and in the fourth, the cause opposite to the previous, namely, the final cause or the good (for this is the end of every generation and every motion). (3:16 Bk A)

The good as final cause becomes the good as an explanatory gnostics. Aristotelian prudence makes moral virtue, as the good within a more ultimate order of things, that which cognition can understand as part of the explication of the experience of that order. The good, both as an explicative experience of knowing and as the explicative knowing of an experience, is an aspect of the intellect whereby thinking comprehends the experiences that lie within an order of things. Cosmology forward is the "thinking of Thinking" by which prudence serves wisdom through a knowing of how any particular order of things in time is part of a more ultimate good that may be within the causality of the universe as a cosmological whole.

Futures As Potentiality And Actuality

An order of things in time is cosmogonic. It is a material expression of cosmological coming-to-be and passing-away. (5) Orders of things in time, as either cosmology forward or cosmology backward, are also the outcomes of potentiality and actuality. Underlying the futures of prudence are the interrelationships of potentiality with actuality. The difference between the two is fundamental for Aristotelian prudence. It is only because of the notion of control that Hobbesian prudence is compelled to take the difference into consideration.

An actuality is that which has been separated out from its whole and exists in its separateness as a something. The existence of a thing is actuality. "Matter exists potentially in view of the fact that it might come to possess a form; and when it exists *actually*, then it exists in a form." (3:155 Bk⊕) An end is also the actuality for which actions are done. "Everything which is being generated proceeds towards a principle and an end. For the final cause (or, that for the sake of which) is a principle, and generation is for the sake of an end, and the end is an *actuality*, and potentiality is viewed as being for the sake of this." (3:155 Bk⊕) Actuality has priority in time over potentiality where actuality is the generative source of a potential thing. "For it is always by a thing in *actuality* that another thing becomes *actualized* from what it was potentially." (3:154 Bk⊕) Actuality as formula is prior in sequence to potentiality in the general meaning of the latter as "every (moving) principle of change or of rest." (3:154 Bk⊕) Actuality as substance is also prior in sequence to potentiality in its general meaning, for it is from "substance that everything which is being generated is being generated from something and by something." (3:154-55 Bk⊕)

Oddly enough, if actuality did not dominate potentiality, there would be neither cosmology backward (Hobbesian prudence) nor cosmology forward (Aristotelian prudence). Actuality and potentiality make the futures of prudence dual futures. If actuality did not so dominate potentiality as to enable a potency or capability to use actuality to pre-emptively regulate potentiality, there could be no control of a future. Yet if actuality was not dominant over potentiality by virtue of its being "prior in substance to potentiality," there would be only the future of cosmology backward.

> The argument is as follows. Every potency is at the same time a potency for the contradictories; for, while that which is not capable of existing could not exist at all, anything which is capable of existing may not be in *actuality*. Thus, that which is capable of existing may or may not exist; and so the same thing is capable of existing and of not existing. And that which has the capability of not existing may not be; and that which may not be is destructible, either without qualification, or with respect to that which it may not be; for example, if in the latter case, it is with respect to place or quantity or quality, but if without qualification, it is with respect to substance. (3:156 Bk⊕)

Contained Futures And The Future As An Abandoned Present

Viewed in terms of control, what is the future that is the cosmology backward of the potency of Hobbesian prudence? It is the containment of potentiality and, as such, a contained future. Felicity as the actuality of the end of prudence is the progress of desire. Given a rational potency of choosing to act on desire, all potentiality not conducive to this end must be contained. Control prevents a potential capability of existing from coming into actuality. Yet felicity as the end of prudential action, is an end that compels designe to bring another and then another actuality into existence. Control is a potency for acting upon matter as potentiality. Control has no function apart from the actuality that is the preference of felicity as the end of prudential action. Felicity is concerned with the actuality of present means whereby to transform them into a potency by which to obtain some apparent future good. Prudence is a potency with respect to designe, and its task as prudence is to function as the potency for taking the pre-materialization of designe as the imagined potentiality of matter and transforming it into an actuality of material form.

Felicity turns upon itself and remains only within itself as the progress of desire in time. There is always a particular something about the matter of the universe as potentiality that must become an actuality of materiality. Felicity compels cosmoplastics without cessation, and is always prior in sequence to potentiality as a principle of change. Felicity makes the future of Hobbesian prudence nothing more than an abandoned present. Felicity, as the actuality of the end of prudence, makes another imaged present the guarantor of an actual present. It does so because that is the way to assure any present actuality against the adverse surprise of potentiality. For each successive present, there is a relevant potency of prudence. There are no alternative futures for felicity, only imagined present actualities of successively realized desires.

All the futures of Hobbesian prudence illustrate futures derived from the priorness of actuality to potency and to principles of change. Here potency can choose from that which exists potentially as matter and choose whether it will be allowed to exist in actuality. The future as an order of things exists actually as a form of matter. The futures of Hobbesian prudence are the futures as to which there is a potency that can choose between their destructibility and their existing. Given this potency for these contradictories, "That which is capable of existing may or may not exist." (3:156 Bk⊕) For Hobbesian prudence, the actuality of the end of action (felicity) introduces both the contained future of control and the future of an abandoned present.

The Intrusive Future of Being

The future of Aristotelian prudence can be brought to the fore and set against the future of Hobbesian prudence. Aristotelian prudence has the potency to generate an intrusive future. An intrusive future is the intrusion of the actuality of Being's "thinking of Thinking" about the future as potentiality. The intrusive future of Being's "thinking of Thinking" about the future is a different manifestation of the Aristotelian position "that *actuality* is prior to potency and to every principle of change." (3:157 Bk⊕)

Being is not a potency. Being is not the materiality of a potency. Being is not the use of potency. Being is not a potency that is actualized in something that is produced. Being, that is to say, does not have performance as its end. "For performance is an end, and *actuality* is performance." (3:155 Bk⊕) Being as whatness is the essence of substance. Being has no function besides its actuality. Being is the actuality of substance. As such, Being, not potency, has priorness.

> But in those cases in which there is no other function besides the *actuality*, the *actuality* exists in that which has it; for example, seeing is in that which sees, investigating is in a man who investigates, and life is in the soul, and so happiness, too, is in the soul (for happiness is a kind of life). And so it is evidence that the *substance* or the form is an *actuality*. According to this argument, then, it is evident that *actuality* is prior in substance to potency; and as we said, one *actuality* always precedes another in time, until we come to the *actuality* of the eternal prime mover. (3:156 Bk⊕)

Here, through Being as prior actuality in substance, is the link between prudence and wisdom. It is a link to a more ultimate order of things than can be imagined by sensibilization alone. The intrusive future of Aristotelian prudence is cosmology forward and manifested in "the thinking of Thinking" of Being. Cosmology forward is rooted in cosmogonic necessity, which cannot exist potentially in the contradictories of a potency of matter as substance.

> For 'necessity' has the following senses: (a) by force, which is contrary to a Thing's tendency, (b) that without which the good is impossible, and (c) that which cannot be otherwise but exists without qualification.
> Such, then, is the principle upon which depends the heaven and

nature. And its *activity* is like the best which we can have but for a little while. For it exists in this manner eternally (which is impossible for us), since its *actuality* is also pleasure. And it is because of this (activity) that being awake, sensing, and Thinking are most pleasant, and hopes and memories are pleasant because of these. Now Thinking according to itself is of the best according to itself, and Thinking in the highest degree is of that which is best in the highest degree. Thus, in partaking of the intelligible, it is of Himself that the Intellect is thinking; for by apprehending and thinking it is he Himself who becomes intelligible, and so the Intellect and its intelligible object are the same. For that which is capable of receiving the intelligible object and the *substance* is the intellect, and the latter is in *actuality* by possessing the intelligible object; so that the possession of the intelligible is more divine than the potency of receiving it, and the contemplation of it is the most pleasant and the best. (3:205 Bk Λ)

The notion of dual futures has now come down to this: The future as the abandoned present and the contained future of control, on the one hand, and the intrusive future, on the other. Desire and the imagination of designe, on the one hand, and Being and "the thinking of Thinking" that is the intelligible, on the other. The reproach of underknowing, on the one hand, and the accusation of overknowing, on the other. Virtue irrelevant future, on the one hand, and virtue relevant future on the other.

Alternate futures are not dual futures. Alternate futures are the outcome of imagic play with analytic or calculative assumptions. Alternate futures are the imagined outcomes of assumptive variants. Alternate futures remain always an imagic content of the pre-materialization of desire and the imagination of designe. They are an aspect of the calculative prelude to the future as the abandonment of the present.

Felicity as an end is but a surrogate for the final end of Hobbesian prudence—which is to achieve a capability like that of cosmology forward. The latter has within it too much mystery for any empirics of sensibilization. Hobbesian prudence backs off from the mystery; warns that it is destructive of empirical knowing. Cosmology forward encompasses all the futures in the universe in all time. The cosmology backward of Hobbesian prudence is focused on more constitutively contained futures in time. Through control it searches for how to narrow down all futures to those contained futures that will be allowed to emerge in time. This is cosmology forward, stripped of its uncontained mystery. The Hobbesian calculative is clever enough by itself, and effective enough when coupled with Hobbesian power, and volitionally regenerative enough as a persistent drive state in the progress of recurrent desire—to achieve the requisite capability level with respect to present means and any future good of desire that is implicit in felicity as an end. Hobbesian prudence, though, backs off from the mystery of cosmology forward; and it remains an unburdened prudence—unburdened by any human interests other than those of felicity and desire itself. It does not take upon itself the burden of the prudence of the Aristotelian strategist—which is the burden of wisdom.

REFERENCES

1. Heisenberg, Werner *Physics and Philosophy*—(Harper & Bros., 1958)
2. Kant, Immanuel *Prolegomena to Any Future Metaphysics*—(1783 Liberal Arts Press ed. 1950, Bobbs-Merrill Inc.)
3. *Aristotle's Metaphysics*—(Hippocrates G. Apostle, Transl. and Comm., Indiana University Press, 1966)
4. *The Nicomachean Ethics of Aristotle*—(F.H. Peters, Transl., Kegan Paul, Trench & Co. London 1884)
5. *Aristotle on Coming-To-Be and Passing-Away*—(E.S. Forster, Transl., Harvard University Press 1955)

BIBLIOGRAPHY

Aristotles' Physics: Books I and II (W. Charlton, Transl., Oxford University Press, 1970)

Aristotle on Coming-To-Be and Passing-Away (Harold H. Joachim, Transl., Intro., and Commentary, Oxford University Press, 1922)

Aristotle on Coming-To-Be and Passing-Away (E.S. Forster, Transl. Harvard University Press, 1955)

Aristotle—Parva Naturalia (W. D. Ross, ed., Oxford University Press, 1955)

Aristotle—De Anima. (R. D. Hicks, Transl. and Notes, Cambridge University Press, 1907)

Aristotle's DeMotu Animalium (Martha C. Nussbaum, Transl., Interp., Comm., Essays, Princeton University Press, 1978)

Aristotle's Metaphysics. (Hippocrates G. Apostle, Transl. and Comm., Indiana University Press, 1966)

Aristotle's Physics (W. D. Ross, Transl. and Comm., Oxford University Press, 1930)

Aristotle's Physics. (Hippocrates G. Apostle, Transl. and Comm., Indiana University Press, 1969)

Bennett, Jonathan. Locke, Berkeley, Hume: Central Themes (Oxford University Press, 1971)

Bergson, Henri. The Creative Mind (Mabelle L. Andison, Transl., Philosophical Library, New York, 1946)

Bergson, Henri. Matter and Memory (Allen and Unwin, London, 1911)

Bergson, Henri. An Introduction to Metaphysics (G.P. Putnam's Sons, New York, 1912)

Bohr, Niels. Atomic Physics and Human Knowledge (John Wiley & Sons, New York, 1958)

Brentano, Frank. On The Several Senses of Being In Aristotle (R. George, Transl., University of California Press, 1975)

Buchanan, E. Aristotle's Theory of Being (University of Mississippi Press, 1962)

Chasis, Herbert and Goldring, William (eds.). Homer William Smith (New York University Press, 1965)

Evans, J.D.G. Aristotle's Physics (W.D. Ross, Transl. and Comm., Oxford University Press, 1930)

Fischer, Kuno. A Commentary on Kant's Critick of The Pure Reason (John P. Mahaffy, Transl., Intro. and Notes, Longmans, Green & Co., 1866)

Flew, Anthony. Hume's Philosophy of Belief (Routledge and Kegan Paul, London, 1961)

Fraser, J. T., Haber, F. C., and Mueller, G. H.—The Study of Time: Proceedings of the First Conference of the International Society for the Study of Time (Springer-Verlag, New York, 1972)

Fraser, J. T., Laurence, N., and Park, D. (eds)—The Study of Time III: Proceedings of the Third Conference of the International Society for the Study of Time (Springer-Verlag, New York, 1978).

Gilson, Etienne. Being and Some Philosophers (Pontifical Institute of Mediaeval Studies, Toronto, Canada, 1949)

Grundstein, Nathan D. The Managerial Kant (Weatherhead School of Management, Case Western Reserve University, Cleveland, Ohio, 1981)

Gunter, P.A.Y. (ed.)—Bergson and the Evolution of Physics (University of Tennessee Press, 1969)

Haldane, E.S. and Ross, G.R.T. (Transl.)—The Philosophical Works of Descartes (Cambridge University Press, 1911 ed. reprint)

Hanson, Norwood Russell. Observation and Explanation (Harper & Row, New York, Torchbook ed., 1971)

Harre, Romano. Matter & Method (Macmillan & Co., Ltd., London, 1964)

Harre, Rom. The Principles of Scientific Thinking (University of Chicago Press, 1970)

Hayek, F. A. Law, Legislation, and Liberty, Vol. I Rules and Order (University of Chicago Press, 1973)

Hayek, F. A. The Sensory Order (Routledge & Kegan Paul, Ltd., London, 1952)

Hayek, F. A. The Counter-Revolution of Science (The Free Press, Glencoe, Ill., 1952)

Heidegger, Martin. Existence and Being (H. Regnery Co., Chicago, 1949)

Heidegger, Martin. Being and Time (John Macquarrie and Edward Robinson, Transl., SCM Press Ltd., London, 1962)

Heidegger, Martin. The End of Philosophy (Joan Stambaugh, Transl., Harper & Row, 1973)
Heidegger, Martin. On Time and Being (Joan Stambaugh, Transl., Harper & Row, New York, 1972)
Heidegger, Martin. The Question Concerning Technology (William Lovitt, Transl. and Intro., Harper & Row, Colophon Books, 1977)
Heidegger, Martin. What Is Called Thinking (Harper & Row, New York, 1968)
Heidegger, Martin. Kant and The Problem of Metaphysics (James S. Churchill, Transl., Indiana University Press, 1962)
Heisenberg, Werner. Physics and Philosophy (Harper and Brothers, New York, 1958)
Heisenberg, Werner. The Physicist's Conception of Nature (Arnold J. Pomerans, Transl., Hutchinson & Co., Ltd., London, 1958)
Henderson, Lawrence J. The Order of Nature (Harvard University Press, 1917)
Hintikka, Jaakko. Time and Necessity: Studies In Aristotle's Theory of Modality (Oxford University Press, 1973)
Hobbes, Leviathan. (Rep. of Ed. of 1651, Oxford University Press, 1909, Imp. of 1929)
The English Works of Thomas Hobbes of Malmesbury (Sir William Molesworth, Ed., John Bohn, London, 11 vols. 1839-1845)
Hume, David. An Inquiry Concerning Human Understanding (edition of 1777) (Charles W. Hendel, Ed. and Intro. Liberal Arts Press, New York, 1955)
Husserl, Edmund. The Phenomenology of Internal Time—Consciousness (Martin Heidegger, Ed., James S. Churchill, Transl., Calvin O. Schrag, Intro., Indiana University Press, 1964)
Kant, Immanuel. The Doctrine of Virtue (M. J. Gregor, Transl. Harper and Row, New York, Torchbook, 1964)
Kant, Immanuel. Prolegomena To Any Future Metaphysics (Lewis White Beck, Ed. and Intro., Liberal Arts Press ed., 1950, Library of Liberal Arts, Bobbs-Merrill, Inc., Indianapolis)
Kant, Immanuel. Critique of Pure Reason (J. M.D. Meiklejohn, Transl. and Intro., Rev. ed., Willey Book Co., New York, 1900)
Langan, Thomas. The Meaning of Heidegger (Columbia University Press, 1959)
Marcel, Gabriel. Presence and Immortality (Michael A. Machado, Transl., Duquesne University Press, Pittsburgh, Pennsylvania, 1967)
Morals of Cicero, The (William Guthrie, Transl. and Intro., London, 1744)

Nicomachean Ethics of Aristotle, The. (F.H. Peters, Transl. Kegan Paul, Trench & Co., London 1884)
Owen, G.E.L. Aristotle on Dialectic (Oxford University Press, 1968)
Paton, H. J. Kant's Metaphysics of Experience, Vol. II (George Allen & Unwin Ltd., London, 1936, Second Imp. 1951)
Price, H. H. Hume's Theory of the External World (Oxford University Press, 1940)
Sallis, John. (Ed. and Intro.)—Heidegger and the Path of Thinking (Duquesne University Press, 1970)
Shepard, Paul. Thinking Animals: Animals and The Development of Human Intelligence (Viking, New York, 1978)
Sorabji, Richard. Aristotle on Memory (Brown University Press, 1972)
Tiryakian, E. A. (ed.)—Sociological Theory, Values, and Socio-Cultural Change (Free Press, Glencoe, 1963)

INDEX

ACTION
world for, 8, 10, 13, 15, 48, 156; and time, 10; theory of Aristotle, 18; Agent of, 32, 48, 94, 136, 137, 157; Material explanation of, 65, 66; Desire and, 66; Acting prudent, 85, 86; and Regulative thought, 71, 132; and deliberation, 76; and change, 114 et. seq.; and being possible, 205; and nature, 108 et. seq., 113, 116, 117; and time-space coding, 121 et. seq.; present and power of action, 131, 132; and sensation, 8, 9, 138, 139; practical action, 140, 141; and matter and force, 159

ACTUALITY
Defined, 164, 165; and Potentiality, 114, 115, 147, 164; and Being, 167; and control, 164, 165; and dual futures, 165; and felicity, 165, 166; and change, 118 et. seq.; world as, 156, 157

APPEARANCE
see Representation; Aristotle and, 28, 65, 66; Sensory, 27, 60; Individuated, 65

BEING
and Prudential knowing, Ch. X
Ontological, 167; Ansensibles, 62, 63; And thought, 65, 96, 160, 161; And an order; And prudence, 97 et. seq.; And gnostics, 98; And time, 98; of the present, 133, 134; and Hobbesian actor, 94, 143, 144; and Aristotelian actor, 144, 145; and Materiality, 142-144; As intrusive future, 166, 167; whatness of, 167; and subjectness, 93, 94; as potency, 96, 97

BEING-IN-THE WORLD, Hobbesian actor, Ch. VIII; Aristotelian actor, Ch. IX, 18, 122, 123

Hobbesian, 40, 103, 78 et. seq.; Competitive, 80; Imagination and, 93, 94; And analytic knowing, 93; And existence, 106, 107; And possessory and non-possessory orders, 91 et. seq.

CALCULATIVE
prudence and, 19, 23; cleverness and, 23, 51, 52; thinking, 99 et. seq.; reasoning, 22; materialization, 104–105; and deliberation, 20, 22, 50, 51; Post-calculative, 77.

CAUSE
and pure strategy; MIN/MAX sense of, 11; and final cause, 11; and time; causal ordering, 129; Triple chain of, 63 et. seq., 82 et. seq.; Hobbesian knowledge of, 11, 12; concept of, 12; Fusing with agency, 12, 13, 126, 133, 137, 160; And regulated thought, 130; And causal inquisitiveness, 124; and temporal order, 125; psychologized causality, 134, 135; ignorance of, 80; sensibilization and, 69; and thought and choice, 147; physics and, 159, 160

CERTITUDE
possessory, 9 et. seq., 135; and world for action, 14, 15; non-possessory and prudence, 20, 21

COGNITION (see THOUGHT, KNOWING)
Strategic, xxxiii et seq.; command, xxxvi; Modality of (Aristotle) xxxiv, 84; Prudential cognition, 50, 51; Post-calculative cognition, 77 et. seq.; Cognized time, 124-126, 127

CONSCIOUSNESS
relation to past/future, 121, 129; Hobbesian, 129 et. seq., 223; percep-

175

tual consciousness and agency, 132-134; and desire, 130, 137; time consciousness (Hobbesian), 150, 151, 153, 156, 130, 132

COSMOLOGY (see)
Futures as, Ch. 16; cosmoplastics, 22, 160; cosmogonics, 23, 160, 164; cosmology forward, 160, 162, 163, 167; Forward/ backward, 160, 165, 168, 169; backward and designe, 161

DELIBERATION
Hobbesian, 11 et. seq., 38, 39, 57; Aristotelian, 19 et. seq., 46 et. seq., 57; and designe, 38; Relation to past/future, 43-45; and prudence, 38 et. seq., 46 et. seq.; and Imagination, 35 et. seq., 139; and purpose, 46, 47, 50, 21, 22; defined, 47, 51, 57; and inquiry, 57; and thought/action, 11, 74, 76

DESIGNE
Hobbesian, 7, 8, 29 et. seq., 38; and desire, 7, 11, 29, 30, 72, 73; as inwardness, 39; as regulative of thought, 42, 44, 96, 97, 7, 8; and deliberation, 40, 44; and imagination, 32, 41, 87, 92, 75, 76; and prudence, 109, 116, 149, 161; and thinking, 173-175, 99-100, 116, 161; and potentiality and futures, 118, 119; and time binding, 122-124; and alternative materialization, 159, 160; and cosmology backwards, 161

DESIRE
Desire itself, 26, 39, 40; Regulative function, 8, 42; object transcendence, 42; and purpose, 53, 54, 59; and designe, see designe; Possessory desire, 30, 32, 74, 135; and past/future, 89, 223 et. seq., 42, 43, 134 et. seq.; Knowledge of, 63; and action, 66; and thought, 66, 67; and reason, 18, 19; cartesian desire, 73; as drive state, 94, 138, 142, 115; and consciousness, 134, 77, 78; and choice, 135; and practical/theoretical, 134; and materialization/ imagination, 156; and felicity, 136, 161

END
and wisdom, 162; Ends/Means and prudence, 18, 20, 39, 52; Ends and virtue, 49; Ends/ Means, 51 et. seq., 22, 23, 140; as actuality, 164

EXPERIENCE
as Hobbesian prudence, 9, 13, 71, 77, 87, 108, 109, 130, 131, 156; as seeing, 20; and memory, 27, 28, 70; equality of, 71; Aristotelian/Hobbesian, 20, 108, 133, 154, 254

FELICITY
defined, 70, 39, 42, 79, 115; and desire, see desire; as actuality, 165, 166; and alternative futures, 168; and cosmology, 168, 169; felicity driven actor, 42

FUTURE
Strategic futures; Futures of pure strategy; Futures making; Future good, 7, 10; Future/past, present, 9, 10; As alternative materialization, 159, 160; Alternative futures, 119, 168, 166; Alternative futures, 119, 168, 166; Intrusive future, 167; Future of prudence, 13, 14, 75-78, 128, 129; Possessive future/past, 39, 42, 135, 136, 142; And desire, 134 et. seq.; And deliberation, 44; Imagined/ presumptive, 43, 44, 136; As a fiction of the mind, 77 et. seq.; Dual futures, 118 et. seq., 168; And regulative duality, 127, 128; Potentiality and futures, 118; As thought, 139; And Aristotelian imagination, 139, 144-146; As practical intellect, 231; As pre-formation, 144, 145; and necessity, 154, 155; As abandoned present, 165, 166, 168; contained futures, 165, 166, 168; As actuality, 166;

GNOSTICS
and virtue, 97, 98, 163, 101 et. seq.; of Being, 96, 97, 98, 104, 94; of Materiality, 95, 98; technologized, 159; and prudential good, 163, 164

GOOD
Hobbesian good and evil, 10, 11, 14-16, 49, 52, 109, 116, 118, 91-92, 109; and Aristotelian virtue, 49 et. seq., 103 et. seq., 23-24; Prudential good, 50, 52 et. seq., 104 et. seq., 231; As principle, 52-54; Apparent good, 53, 54; Good, Aristotelian, 47 et. seq., 54, 101 et. seq.; Order and, 163, 104 et. seq.; Moral goodness, 97; and practical action, 140-142; and potentiality/actuality, 118

IMAGINATION
As thought, 34-36, 44, 28, 29, 142; Hobbesian, 36, 43-45, 26 et. seq., 143, 84, 226; Aristotelian, 33 et. seq., 138-140, 144 et. seq.; Deliberative, 35, 139, 140; Transcendent, 36, 37; Empirical, 36, 30, 32, 27, 28; and past/future, 43-45,

Index

136, 139; Practical imagination, 44; and prudence, 41; as formative capability, 77, 85, 87 et. seq.; and designe, 147, 41, 72-74, 87 et. seq.; and being-in-the-world, 88, 93, 94

KNOWING
Prudential, 9, 10, 60, 61, 83, 86, Ch. X, 31, 124, 99-100; of desire, 63; overknowing/underknowing, 163, 172, 83 et. seq., 93, 99, 100; Aristotle, modes of, 84; and Materiality, 85, 88, 92; of non-possessory order, 90, 91; Preferential knowledge, 92; Interrogative knowledge, 92; And Being-in-the-world, 93; Analytic knowing, 93; and virtue, 97, 98, 102 et. seq., 180; actual and potential knowledge, 34; sensory knowledge, 30 et. seq.; of causality, 149 et. seq., 163, 12, 13; and Being, Ch. X

MATERIALITY
Strategy and material reality, see Preface; of explanation; Aristotle/Hobbes, 142 et. seq.; Alternative materialization, 160; psychologizing of; world of, 8, 156; and matter, 60 et. seq., 146, 147; and action, 65, 66; triple chain of, 68 et. seq.; and sensibilization, 69; and subjectivity, 72 et. seq.; backward/forward, 72; Three questions of (Hobbesian), 82 et. seq.; Cartesian materiality, 123; nonmateriality of past/present, 124 et. seq.; and the future, 139, 146; Kinematic/Kinetic materiality, 146, 147; and order, 154 et. seq.; of thought, 157; and desire/imagination, 157

MATTER
doctrines of, 114 et. seq.; physics and, et. seq.; as form/substance, 60 et. seq.; Intelligible matter, 96, 34, 35, 88, 90; and change, 118, 119; and materiality, 141 et. seq., 96, 97; and potentiality/actuality, 118, 119, 147, 113-115

MEDITATIVE
as thought, 101 et. seq.; and unconcealment, 101, 105, 106; and Passionless Thought, 101, 102

MEMORY
and experience, 27, 28, 121, 134, 111, 31, 44; Aristotelian/Hobbesian, 110 et. seq., 124; and recollection, 124, 125, 110 et. seq.; and past, 129, 110

NATURE
and man, 62; and purpose, serving events, 109 et. seq., 116; and telic causality, 113 et. seq.; Aristotelian/Hobbesian, 112 et. seq., 155 et. seq.; and action, 108 et. seq., 116, 117; and substance, 61, 62

ORDER (see POSSESSORY)
and pure strategy, xli; Temporality of, 154 et seq.

PAST
and desire, 42, 43, 39; and imagination, 43; and deliberation, 43, 83; and non-materiality, 128; as powerlessness, 128 et. seq.; as consciousness, 129, 130; as expectation, 130, 131, 13, 14

POSSESSORY
stance, 63, 70, 71, 135; imagination, 8; certitude, 9 et. seq., 14; non-possessory certitude, 20, 21; desire, 8, 29, 30, 32, 135; future/ past, 39, 42, 131, 225; order, 88, 93, 94, 163; non-possessory order, 91, 92

POTENCY
Aristotelian, 85 et. seq.; Cartesian and Hobbesian, 70 et. seq.; Hobbesian, 87; as inequalities, 71; and designe, 77, 78, 70; and subjectivity, 71 et. seq.; and power of present means, 83; and the future, 39, 40; and time, 73 et. seq.; Formative Potency, 88;

PRUDENCE
conceptions of and Philosophies of Foreword and Ch. I; Burdened, unburdened, 169, 161, 162; Prudentiality of, Ch. I; Aristotelian, Ch. III; Hobbesian, Ch. II; And virtue, 23, 24, 49 et. seq., 97, 98, 102 et. seq.; And wisdom, 24, 161, 162, 169; and calculation, see Reason; and certitude, see Possessory; As capability, 21, 22, 70, 71; As Other-Than-Action, Ch. IV-VI; As experience, 31, 69, 70, 77, 130, 131; As judgment, 44; And imagination, designe, deliberation, 38 et. seq.; Prudential deliberation, 45 et. seq.; Prudential cognition, 77 et. seq.; Prudential good, 52 et. seq.; and cleverness, 51, 52; And dialectic, 57, 58 et. seq.; And counsel, 58, 59; and moral goodness, 104, 107, 162, 163; and seeing, 99, 100, 106, 107, 102, 116; and unconcealment, 101, 102; and designe, 109, 149, 161, 7; and Hobbesian world-

177

hood, 108 et. seq.; and time, 124 et. seq., 149 et. seq.; and Hobbesian/Aristotelian Thinking, 159 et. seq.; and potentiality/actuality, 114 et. seq., 164, 165

REASON
Hobbesian, 15, 76, 77; Reason Itself; Contemplative reason; Right reason, 15, 52, 107; Desire and reason, 23, 18, 19; Cleverness and practical reason, 51, 52; Reason as reckoning, 74, 75, 96, 97, 99; Reason and calculation, 76, 77, 100, 101, 104, 105, 22, 49, 106, 19; Practical reason, 86, 87, 141, 142, 23; Rational powers/ Aristotelian, 22, 24, 86, 142 et. seq.

SENSIBILIZATION
of thought, 28 et. seq., 6, 7, 118, 119, 142; and strategic cognition, 143 et. seq.; sensation and memory, 17; Aristotelian sensibilization, 17, 33, et. seq, 65 et. seq.; and causality, 69, 70, 108, 109; sensory present/past, 27, 43; sensory sequence, 28, 108; sensory knowledge, 60 et. seq.; sensory cognition and time, 124-127, 132 et. seq.

SENSIBLES
matter as empty sensible, 61; and Substance, 62, 63

STRATEGIST
and history of thought, 11-12; as causal agent, 109, 112, 115-116, 123-124, 149-150; as Hobbesian Actor, 122-123, 112-113; as Aristotelian Actor, et. seq.

STRATEGY
Defined, 30; pure strategy, theory of, Preface; pure and practical, xxvii–xxviii; and materiality, xxix et seq.; and causality, agency and time, xxxi et seq.; and cognition, xxxiii et seq.; Aristotelian strategist, xxxv-xxxvii, xlii, xlv; Hobbesian strategist, xxxviii, xlii, xliv; and being, xxxix-xl; futures of pure strategy, xl et seq.; and an order, xli; and reason, xlii-xliv

SUBJECTIVITY
subjectness, 72 et. seq.; reciprocal, 54-56; and felicity, 55; itself, 54-56; and virtue, 54-55; Hobbesian, 75, 78, 142; as prematerialization, 72-73, 78; and thought, 73-74; and passions, 71-73

THINKING (see THOUGHT, COGNITION)
and representation, 66-67; and Being, 95-97; fateful thinking, 98-99; calculative thinking, 99-101, 104-105; and designe, 100-101; that sees, 98 et. seq.; reflective thinking, 102; Passionate/meditative thinking, 101 et. seq., 105; Thinking Animals, 121-122

THOUGHT (See Cognition, Knowing)
Imagination as thought, 34-37; as final cause; and attributes of materiality; As a power; Prudential thought, 74 et. seq.; Hobbesian thought, 36-37, Ch. II; Desire and designe as regulative of, 6-8, 35-36, 38-39, 44, 40-42, 70, 73; Enmattered thought, 30 et. seq.; Aristotelian thought, 65-66; Regulated by practical imagination, 44; Strategy of, Ch. VII; and being, 62-63, Ch. X; Sensibilization and thought, Ch. II, Ch. III, 69; And possessory stance, 9-10, 70; and action, 71, 131-132, 140; and time and desire, 73 et. seq.; and subjectivity, 72, 75-76; and representation, 66-67, 138-139, 144, 96; Future as thought, 139-140, 115; and choice, 147; Trayne of thought, Ch. II, 70, 109; Regulated, 6, 146, 28-30, 70-71, 117, 132-133, 146, 157

TIME
Times of time, Ch. XV; framework of time, 9; event time, 63, 150-151, 153, 108; psychological now, 62-65, 124-126, 150-151; Aristotelian Now, 64, 145; Volitional time, 98-99, 151, 153; Temporal order, 153-155, 125-126, 108, 113, 123; Space-time binding, 108-109; Time-binding, 121, 124; Time-space coding, 121 et. seq.; Cognized time, 124-126; Intentive time, 126-127; Timing behavior, 126-127; Psychological time, 132-134; Aristotelian/Hobbesian present, 143-144, 153; Heterogenic/Homogenic time, 149-150; And Prudence, 149 et. seq., 154, 151; Augustinian concept of, 150; Hobbesian time consciousness, 129 et. seq.; Social time, 152-153; Relationality and time, 151-152, 124-125, and logical naturalism, 153; and orderless temporality, 156 et. seq.

VIRTUE
and wisdom, 4; relation to vice, 49-50; and the good, 52-54; and character, 56;

Index

Prudence and, 4, 46, 49 et. seq., 97-98, 102-103; Hobbesian, 49, 83; and ends 51-52; and possessory order, 88, 92; relation to designe and action, 89; and gnostics, 97-98; and thought and knowing, 102 et seq.

VOLITION
and purpose, 21-22; reaction to mechanism, 36; and liberty, 11, 41, 74; willed acts, 46-48; and time, 98-99, 149 et seq.

WISDOM
and prudence, 4, 24, 161-162, 169

WORLDHOOD
with/without nature, Ch. XI

WORLD
Pure exteriority of, 10-12, 137; and possessory certitude, 9 et. seq.; as sensory actuality, 156-157; as materially sensibilized, 8, 68-69; and possessory stance, 70, 135; being-in-(Hobbesian), 78 et. seq., 123, 131, 133-134; psychologizing of, 134; alternative materialization of 159-160